CHOICE Books
for College Libraries

CHOICE Books for College Libraries

Reviews of Publications from The Edwin Mellen Press

Compiled by Toni Tan

The Edwin Mellen Press
Lewiston . Queenston . Lampeter

Library of Congress Cataloging-in-Publication Data

This book has been registered with the Library of Congress.

CHOICE Books for College Libraries
Reviews of Publications from The Edwin Mellen Press

Compiled by Toni Tan

ISBN 0-7734-6163-9

A CIP catalog record for this book is available from the British Library.

The Edwin Mellen Press
Box 450
Lewiston, New York
USA 14092-0450
Tel: (716) 754-2266
Fax: (716) 754-4056
Email:info@mellenpress.com

The Edwin Mellen Press
Box 67
Queenston, Ontario
CANADA L0S 1L0
Tel:(866) MELLENP
Fax: (716) 754-4056
Email:info@mellenpress.com

The Edwin Mellen Press, Ltd.
17 Lampeter Industrial Estates
Lampeter, Ceredigion, Wales
UNITED KINGDOM SA48 8LT
Tel: 44 1570 423 356
Fax: 44 1570 423 775
Email:emp@mellen.demon.co.uk

www.mellenpress.com

Printed in Canada

Titles from The Edwin Mellen Press in representative libraries worldwide

Harvard University	3,233
University of Toronto	2,857
University of North Carolina	2,359
Princeton University	2,033
Stanford University	1,857
Biblioteca nacional (Madrid)	1,831
Oxford University	1,811
National Library of Sweden	889
Bibliothèque nationale de France	759
Melbourne Library (Australia)	626

*Statistics as of August 2002

We wish to thank
the American Library Association
for permission to reprint
these reviews from CHOICE.

PREFACE

The Association of College and Research Libraries publishes a journal, CHOICE, whose mission is to review and recommend books for college library acquisition.

This volume comprises over 100 CHOICE recommendations of books published by The Edwin Mellen Press. Each review has been reproduced in its entirety without any editing.

CHOICE also selects, from the 20,000 books it reviews annually, a small number as "Outstanding Academic Titles". Publications from The Edwin Mellen Press have received this honor in previous years.

This year, *The Evolution of the Liberal Democratic State with a Case Study of Latinos in San Antonio, Texas* by Henry Flores was commended by CHOICE as one of its Outstanding Academic Titles.

Toni Tan, M.B.A.
Compiler

Note: For further information about these and all other titles by The Edwin Mellen Press, please visit www.mellenpress.com.

Contents

Contents

CHOICE Books
for College Libraries

selected by
CHOICE

Outstanding Academic Title

THE EVOLUTION OF
THE LIBERAL DEMOCRATIC STATE WITH
A CASE STUDY OF LATINOS IN
SAN ANTONIO, TEXAS

by Henry Flores

0-7734-6674-6   248pp.   2003

Flores (St. Mary's University) shows a masterful command of the literature on the theory of the state in this example of outstanding scholarship. The most significant contribution of this volume is the application of chaos theory from the natural sciences, which creates a broad theoretical framework to better understand both theories of the state and Latino and American politics. In reminding readers of the paramount role of the nexus of the private and public sectors, associated impact of ideology, and the nature of a structured liberal democratic American state, Flores demonstrates, despite the seemingly dynamic and responsive nature of the state, why Latinos may very well continue to realize potentially overwhelming obstacles and resistance to full and real political participation in useful public policy development in the US. Very useful preface, index, and impressive bibliography. **Summing Up:** Highly recommended. Undergraduate and graduate students, researchers, faculty, and policy makers. -- *A. A. Sisneros, University of Illinois at Springfield*
Review in 2004 May CHOICE

selected by
CHOICE

Outstanding Academic Title

THE SOCIOLOGY OF LAW:
A BIBLIOGRAPHY OF THEORETICAL LITERATURE
(2nd Edition)

by A. Javier Treviño

0-7734-8318-7   220pp.   1998

Treviño's superb bibliography is organized around themes
that place the theoretical literature of the sociology of law
in both historical context and comparative perspective.
The table of contents reads like a wonderful course out-
line. The first heading indicates that the materials deal
with definitional problems within the concept of law and
the sociology of law; subsequent headings identify major
schools of sociolegal thought, and subheadings treat leading figures or subschools of thought. To his credit, the author has not sought to be comprehensive in his bibliographical coverage, but has used excellent judgment in
selecting a relatively small number of the best and most
enduring articles in each area. This will prevent the book
from becoming dated for some time. Anyone teaching a
theoretically inclined course in the sociology of law could
easily turn the table of contents into a syllabus, then con-
struct a set of readings for the course by selecting articles
listed under each topic. This bibliography should be of
immense value to scholars, and to students who want to
quickly locate major writings on major topics in the field.
Despite its value for bibliographical reference on a
scholar's bookshelf, works like this should be among the
earliest candidates for electronic publication. -- *M. M.
Feeley, University of California, Berkeley*
Review in 1999 Mar CHOICE

selected by
CHOICE

Outstanding Academic Title

A POLITICAL APPROACH TO PACIFISM

by Will Morrisey

Vol. 1: 0-7734-8910-X   472pp.   1996
Vol. 2: 0-7734-8910-X   460pp.   1996

Massively erudite, this work argues against absolute pacifism and "bellicism" in favor of "prudent" just-war fighting by "'American' commercial republics" into the indefinite future. Research support from the US Institute for Peace is acknowledged. The text is contained in v.1 (451 p.) and requires reference to v.2, which consists entirely of 2,229 extensive endnotes (216 p.), more than 1,500 bibliographical sources (95 p.), and a name index (37 p.). Inspired by Plato's dialogic Republic, explicitly emulated in chapter 4, Morrisey reviews arguments from antiquity to the present. His critical interpolations throughout emphasize grounds for rejection of pacifism that will be familiar to readers of this work: human nature is prone to lethal aggression; defensive killing for survival of self, society, and freedom is justified. Morrisey's uniquely comprehensive work summarizes and carries forward the long tradition of justifications for war and violence in Western political philosophy. As Leon Harold Craig notes in his study of Plato's Republic, "there is a deep relationship between philosophy and war" (The War Lover, CH, Apr'95). Recommended for war and peace collections, advanced researchers, and admirers of scholarly erudition. -- *G. D. Paige, emeritus, University of Hawaii at Manoa*
Review in 1996 Oct CHOICE

reviewed by
CHOICE

Recommended
Titles

A Social History of the Bakwena and Peoples of the Kalahari of Southern Africa, 19th Century

by Gary Y. Okihiro

0-7734-7839-6   220pp.   2000

The Bakwena, living on the edge of Botswana's Kalahari Desert, have a complex history, one little known to ethnographers and historians of southern Africa. Based on archival sources and interviews with hundreds of Bakwena during 1975, Okihiro reconstructs their movements, fissions and fusions, rise and fall of chieftaincies, trading alliances, changing household formations, and subsistence practices during the 19th century. In-depth genealogies, the core of Okihiro's data, provide insight into political, communal, and household groupings, which were significantly modified through immigrations from outside and relations with others living in the Kalahari. The final chapter describes Bakwena relationships with Christian missionaries and white traders. Although Okihiro's ethnography is not grounded in contemporary ethnographic theory and historical issues of southern African, a vast quantity of data is made available for the first time. Upper-division undergraduates and above. -- *K. M. Weist, University of Montana*
Review in 2000 July CHOICE

THE INTERRELATEDNESS OF MUSIC, RELIGION, AND RITUAL IN AFRICAN PERFORMANCE PRACTICE

Edited by Daniel K. Avorgbedor

0-7734-6821-8   464pp.   2003

Avorgbedor (Ohio State Univ.) divides the 12 essays in this insightful volume into four sections. After the introduction (part 1), the content turns to indigenous religious and ritual practices, where one finds, for example, "Gods and Deputy Gods," Akin Euba's discussion of the Yoruba, and "Performance as Ritual, Performance as Art," in which Diane Thram looks at an indigenous form of sacred ritual music and dance as it moved from ritual to performing art. Gerhard Kubik's contribution to this section, "Mukanda: Boys' Initiation in Eastern Angola," seems out of place and outdated because it relies on dated research (1965-87) yet refers to the present. Section 3, on healing and performance, comprises four essays, including Moya Aliya Malamusi's "Identifying Witches," which discusses a medical practitioner in Malawi, and "Where All Things Meet," Barbara Thompson's discussion of Shambaa healing. Section 4, on the integration of Christianity into the lives of Africans and African Americans, includes such contributions as Thomasina Neely-Chandler's "Modes of Ritual Action and Performance in African-American Pentecostalism." Including 20 photographs (some in color), several appendixes (music transcriptions), and a helpful bibliography, this volume will serve collections supporting performance studies, cultural studies, and African and African American studies. An index would have been helpful. **Summing Up:** Recommended. Graduate students and above. -- *E. C. Ramirez, formerly, St. Philip's College* ***Review in 2004 Nov CHOICE***

STATE AND RELIGION IN THE SUDAN: SUDANESE THINKERS

by Mahgoub El-Tigani Mahmoud

0-7734-6748-3   392pp.   2003

The theme of the interaction of religious sectarianism, Islam, and Islamism, and regional and ethnic identities is central to an analysis of the Sudan, as these two books demonstrate, although in different ways. Warburg, an Israeli academic with numerous articles and books on the Nile Valley and Islam (e.g., *Historical Discord in the Nile Valley*, CH, Jun'93), writes clearly and effectively "that in Sudan Islam and politics were so intertwined that they could not be separated" and stresses "the overwhelming power of sectarianism" in comprehending the tangled evolution of the Sudan. His book represents a condensation or culmination of decades of research and publication, and is thus of significant value as a well-written and authoritative analysis of the Sudan from the 19th-century Mahdiyya to the contemporary, troubled Islamist state (see also Ann Lesch, *The Sudan: Contested Natural Identities*, 1998).

Mahmoud (sociology, Tennessee State Univ.) is a Sudanese academic in exile because of his liberal reformist views of Islam and human rights in his home country. His manuscript conveying the anguish of a proud and hopeful national scholar was smuggled out of the Sudan, published in Cairo in Arabic, and has now been translated into English with a complementary foreword by Carolyn Fluehr-Lobban, an anthropologist specializing in the Sudan. In contrast to Warburg's more chronological analysis of the last two centuries, Mahmoud's volume is a more specialized and personalized interpretation of the same overall topic. It focuses especially on four prominent Sudanese religious-political-intellectual thinkers (Hassan al-Turabi, Abd al-Khaliq Mahgoub, Sadiq al-Mahdi, and Mahmoud Mohammed Taha) and on the author's thoughtful analysis of how these men have sought to come to terms with religious traditions and contemporary circumstances, though not necessarily in the liberal democratic direction favored by the author. **Summing Up:** Recommended. Warburg, larger public libraries and upper-division undergraduates and above; Mahmoud, faculty and researchers. -- *B. Harris Jr., Occidental College*
Review in 2004 Mar CHOICE

PAN-AFRICAN EDUCATION: THE LAST STAGE OF EDUCATIONAL DEVELOPMENTS IN AFRICA

by John K. Marah

0-88946-186-4   348pp.   1989

This bold and challenging study (Volume 2 in the "Studies in African Education" series) focuses on the potential use of "Pan African Education"--a system that espouses education for "all"--as an educational process that could bring about and perpetuate African unity or a "United African States." Marah, an African of Sierra Leonian heritage, reviews traditional and Western education in African settings and then explains how Africa's educational institutions, teachers, and politicians have perpetuated the unfulfilled concept of African unity. He then illustrates how that unity can materialize through the development of African educational institutions designed to achieve African unity and integration. Schools would be integrated, the curriculum would be changed to fit the principles of African unity, African teachers would be trained in integrated settings, and an all-African university would be instituted. Marah believes that Pan African educational institutions would be "authentic" development and research oriented institutions that "would also create political, social, economic, and psychological attitudes that would revolutionize African economies, politics and social psychology." The book presents interesting ideas and concepts. Extensive chapter notes, and an excellent selected bibliography. Recommended for upper-division undergraduates and above. -- *R. Adesiyan, Purdue University--Calumet Campus*

Review in 1990 Feb CHOICE

A NARRATIVE BIBLIOGRAPHY OF THE AFRICAN-AMERICAN FRONTIER: BLACKS IN THE ROCKY MOUNTAIN WEST, 1535-1912

by Roger D. Hardaway

0-7734-8879-0   252pp.   1996

Hardaway's annotated bibliography is a slight revision of his doctoral dissertation, taking into account secondary sources published through the first half of 1994. The geographical scope (the Rocky Mountain West) includes the states of Arizona, Colorado, Idaho, Montana, Nevada, New Mexico, Utah, and Wyoming. The time span extends from 1535, when Estevanico, the first African slave, reportedly traveled through the region, to 1912, when the territories of Arizona and New Mexico became states. The cited sources include more than 50 books and 150 articles taken from 62 journals. Each entry has a complete bibliographic citation and a lengthy annotation. The 15 topical chapters cover general studies, Estevanico, the Spanish colonial frontier, York (an African American member of the Lewis and Clark expedition), mountain men, slavery, blacks and Mormons, the mining frontier, the military frontier, buffalo soldiers, cowboys, women, farmers and ranchers, the urban frontier, and discrimination. Most chapters end with a section of materials appropriate for adolescents. There are indexes for state, journal, subject (name), and author. Recommended for academic libraries with research collections in African American and Rocky Mountain West history. -- *P. A. Frisch, Washington and Jefferson College*
Review in 1996 May CHOICE

ALEXANDER CRUMMELL (1819-1898) AND THE CREATION OF AN AFRICAN-AMERICAN CHURCH IN LIBERIA

by J.R. Oldfield

0-88946-074-4   165pp.   1990

Alexander Crummell (1819-1898) was a leading African-American intellectual, nationalist, pan-Africanist, Episcopal minister, and emigrationist who became a role model for W.E.B. DuBois by wrestling with the paradoxes of being black in America. Oldfield's slight, readable book summarizes Crummell's life but focuses on his attempt to found a national church in Liberia. The enterprise failed because of the obtuseness of white colonial church administrators, the black-mulatto color-caste split in Liberia itself, and Crummell's own austere, aristocratic, and authoritarian personality. Crummell's great contribution was his effort to define how blacks could claim their full rights as American citizens while maintaining an African presence in the New World. His complex life and thought are more completely examined in Wilson J. Moses's Alexander Crummell: A Study of Civilization and Discontent (1989) and Gregory Rigsby's Alexander Crummell: Pioneer in Nineteenth-Century Pan-African Thought (CH, Jun'87). Undergraduate and public libraries. -- *R. Newman, New York Public Library*
Review in 1990 Sept CHOICE

Voice in the Slave Narratives of Olaudah Equiano, Frederick Douglass, and Solomon Northrup

by Carver Wendell Waters

0-7734-6988-5   252pp.   2002

Waters (Savannah State Univ.) provides a thorough literary history of the use and variety of voice among Africans and African Americans. For example, he delves into the African oral tradition and its relationship to the American slave narrative custom of the 18th and 19th centuries. The depth of the analysis in terms of its historical implications and its literary connections is sobering. The autobiographies Waters looks at presented an opportunity for African Americans to "write themselves into existence" and thereby "exert their humanity in a society that, more often than not, regarded them as mere mules." Autobiographers such as Equiano, Douglass, and Northrup harnessed the power of the spoken as well as the written word in order to achieve physical and psychological freedom in the US. Waters found a treasure trove of information in dissertations--an unusual source for established scholars to mine--and uses it to advantage. Finally, although typos are distracting, this study not only offers a meticulous discussion of three significant narratives but also presents a full scholarly critique of these manuscripts. **Summing Up:** Recommended. Lower-division undergraduates through faculty. -- *C. N. Ijeoma, Pennsylvania State University, Abington Campus*
Review in 2003 June CHOICE

THE COLLECTED WRITINGS OF JESSIE FORSYTH, 1847-1937: THE GOOD TEMPLARS AND TEMPERANCE REFORM ON THREE CONTINENTS

Edited by David M. Fahey

0-88946-296-8   528pp.   1988

Few Americans have heard of the Independent Order of Good Templars, though they may be quite aware of the temperance movement, the fight for national Prohibition, the Women's Christian Temperance Union, and the Anti-Saloon League. Yet the Order, organized in New York State in 1851, claimed over 500,000 members in North America by 1868. Fahey (Miami University--Ohio) brings the Templars to life with a nicely edited collection of the writings of Jessie Forsythe (1847-1937), a Good Templar member and officer from 1872 until her death. An Englishwomen who lived in the US from 1875 to 1911, Forsyth made the Order her life. She was involved in the international split over racial policies in the US, and was a fighter for greater acceptance of women as leaders in the European organizations. Forsyth was interested in Bella-myite ideas, and passionately committed to the education of children in temperance issues. Her life exemplified the ability of Good Templar lodges to provide members with an attractive combination of dedication to the goal of total abstinence in a social setting designed to promote individual growth, self-help, and bonds of friendship. Following a clear and helpful 67-page introduction, Fahey presents Forsyth's writings, which include her memoirs, essays, letters, and fiction. Carefully recounting surface events, Forsyth does not reveal much of her motives, personal crises, or psychology. One is left interested but wishing to know much more. Upper-division undergraduates and above. -- *J. P. Felt, University of Vermont*
Review in 1989 May CHOICE

AMERICA, PHILANTHROPY, AND THE MORAL ORDER

by John H. Hamer

0-7734-7067-0   216pp.   2002

Hamer is trained as an anthropologist and appears to be new to the study of philanthropy. His book reviews some of the major literature but appears to have neglected many of the standard and major works, both books and articles. Nevertheless, he has brought together well-known information about 13 diverse philanthropists (and "non-philanthropists"), and he tells an interesting story about what he perceives as the decline of the community-oriented philanthropy of the great era of philanthropy a century or more ago in comparison with the business-dominated and self-interested philanthropy of the present day. He also provides brief but interesting comparisons of US philanthropy with the somewhat comparable practices of nonindustrialized peoples. Hamer's scheme is highly formalistic, and his command of the historical narrative is not that of a professional historian. But his book is generally well written and will interest those who want to see an alternative view of the subject. **Summing Up:** Optional. Suitable for public libraries. -- *S. N. Katz, Princeton University*
Review in 2003 Mar CHOICE

THE TRANSFORMATION OF ARIZONA INTO A MODERN STATE: THE CONTRIBUTION OF WAR TO THE MODERNIZATION PROCESS
by Charles Ynfante

0-7734-7206-1   216pp.   2002

Ynfante (Mesa Technical College) describes Arizona's participation in the war effort in this book that makes an important contribution as a state study of the home front in WW II. He provides an overview of developments before, during, and immediately after the war years. His book has two themes. The first deals with Arizona's institutions and their development as a direct result of the war; the second deals with the effects of the war on the state's ethnic groups. Ynfante argues that as elsewhere in the West, WW II helped create a modern, diversified economy that was no longer dependent on extractive and agricultural products. On the other hand, he concludes that the war did not hasten social integration by breaking down barriers that discriminated against racial and ethnic minorities. His book is thoroughly researched, using both primary and secondary sources, and is arranged topically while treating important events chronologically. For further reading see Gerald D. Nash's *The American West Transformed: The Impact of the Second World War* (CH, Oct'85). General and academic collections. -- *R. E. Marcello, University of North Texas*
Review in 2003 Jan CHOICE

DEFINING AMERICAN INDIAN LITERATURE: ONE NATION DIVISIBLE

by Robert L. Berner

0-7734-8039-0   164pp.   1999

Berner (emeritus, Univ. of Wisconsin, Oshkosh) analyzes the place of American Indian literature in the context of US literary traditions. Covering subjects ranging from the cultural identity of the writer to literary use of Native American themes to Native writers' debt to other literatures, the work includes detailed readings from various genres and discussion of cultural and historical issues. Not everyone will approve of the author's choice of texts: he selects some that are marginal to Native American literature and shortchanges some generally considered classics (e.g., Berner's discussion of Black Elk's life history concentrates almost entirely on numerical repetition). In addition, Berner is not clear about where his discussion is leading. Not until the last chapter does he articulate the conclusion that Native American literature must be seen as a unique and inseparable part of all literatures in the US rather than as a literature with boundaries in opposition to other US literatures. Outspoken and sometimes "testy" about other critics, Berner has written a thought-provoking, stimulating volume for graduate students, researchers, and faculty in the field. -- *B. Hans, University of North Dakota*
Review in 2000 Feb CHOICE

A CONCORDANCE TO THE COMPLETE WORKS OF ANNE BRADSTREET: A SPECIAL EDITION OF STUDIES IN PURITAN AMERICAN SPIRITUALITY

by Craig A. Raymond

0-7734-7814-0   648pp.   2000

Craig's exhaustive work of scholarship is not really appropriate for undergraduate collections. The author reproduces every word and every variant spelling in Anne Bradstreet's poetry and prose, and provides the accompanying line or partial line in which that word occurs. Because there is no standard edition of all Bradstreet's work, the concordance uses a somewhat cumbersome but workable combination of references to several different works and their line numbers. For scholars who need to know every occurrence of the word "did" in Bradstreet's work, the line in which it is used, and the times she used "did'st" or "didst" (ten pages of citations to these three words), this set will be the work they want. But "pricey" is an understatement, and why the volumes are individually priced is a mystery: would one want only the volume that covers A-M? If one has access to *Literature Online* (http://lion.chadwyck.com/html/homenosub.htm) (originally created by Chadwyck-Healey), one would not need this book, at least for Bradstreet's poetry. Use of a Kurzweil machine and specialized software (called PC-Case) made this book possible. Whether it is really necessary is another question; one can only hope those who spoof academia never discover it. Research collections. --
W. Miller, Florida Atlantic University
Review in 2001 Jan CHOICE

An Annotated Walt Whitman Bibliography, 1976-1985

by Brent Gibson

0-7734-7577-X   336pp.   2001

One of many contributors to the excellent *Walt Whitman: An Encyclopedia*, ed. by J.R. LeMaster and Donald D. Kummings (CH May'99), Gibson offers in this bibliography a revision of his PhD dissertation. It complements previous bibliographies by Scott Giantvalley (*Walt Whitman, 1836-1939: A Reference Guide*, CH, Apr'82) and Kummings (*Walt Whitman, 1940-1975: A Reference Guide*, CH, Mar'83), and the "Current Bibliographies" printed in *Walt Whitman Review* and its successor *Walt Whitman Quarterly Review*, which are also available at *Walt Whitman: A Current Bibliography* (http://jefferson.village.virginia.edu/whitman/bib/index.html). The decade of Whitman scholarship Gibson documents witnessed, among other things, a sustained critical interest in psychoanalytic approaches to Whitman, increased interest in Whitman and homosexuality, and increased critical attention to Whitman's markedly dark "As I Ebb'd with the Ocean of Life" (1880). The bibliography's 900 English-language entries contain succinct annotations that "are largely nonevaluative summaries adopting the point of view of the work being annotated." Grouped by year, then arranged alphabetically by author, the entries cite works--including book reviews, revised works, and PhD dissertations, but excluding reprints and master's and undergraduate theses--that Gibson believes added significantly to the scholarship on Whitman. Interesting but perhaps less useful is a brief section citing works about Whitman in languages other than English, which unfortunately lacks annotations. Recommended for academic libraries. -- *W. D. Walsh, University of New Hampshire*
Review in 2001 Oct CHOICE

THE FEMINIZED MALE CHARACTER IN TWENTIETH-CENTURY LITERATURE

by Nancy McCampbell Grace

0-7734-8998-3   312pp.   1995

Grace employs sociological and psychoanalytical theory to describe the shifting perceptions and changing definitions of masculinity in 20th-century writing by men, as she discusses the "conflict between prescriptions for behavior that force us into social roles, and the imagination and sexual instinct." She explores the conscious and unconscious impulses that led to the creation of James Joyce's Leopold Bloom, Ernest Hemingway's Jake Barnes, Jack Kerouac's Sal Paradise, and Saul Bellow's Charlie Citrine--characters whose creators diverged from cultural criteria of the "true" man and imbued their male characters with attributes the culture characterizes as feminine. Though suggesting that Hemingway took the greatest risks in exploring the psychic and social dimensions of gender reformation in The Garden of Eden, the author acknowledges those critics who suggest that the feminized male sometimes leaves women with little or nothing of their own. Perhaps more could be made of this important point, particularly in the work of the male writers discussed here. A worthy addition to the growing literature on gendered reading, this work is a strong companion to Judith Fetterley's The Resisting Reader (CH, Mar'79) and Carolyn Heilbrun's Toward a Recognition of Androgyny (CH, Oct'73). All academic collections. -- *L. Winters, College of Saint Elizabeth*
Review in 1995 Nov CHOICE

Biography of American Author Jean Toomer, 1894-1967

by John Chandler Griffin

0-7734-7088-3   248pp.   2002

The result of almost 30 years of research and writing, this volume does not so much break new ground in Toomer scholarship as embellish existing knowledge about this enigmatic figure. When Griffin (emer., Univ. of South Carolina) began his research, scholarly work on Toomer consisted almost exclusively of Darwin Turner's *In a Minor Chord: Three Afro-American Writers and Their Search for Identity* (CH, Apr'73). After Nellie McKay published *Jean Toomer, Artist* (CH, Jan'85), however, studies about Toomer have grown apace and now include Rudolph Byrd's *Jean Toomer's Years with Gurdjieff* (CH, Sep'91), Jon Woodson's *To Make a New Race* (CH, Dec'99), and *Jean Toomer and the Harlem Renaissance*, ed. by Geneviève Fabre and Michel Feith (CH, Sep'01). Griffin's contribution to this ongoing conversation rests on his extensive mining of Toomer's papers and his personal acquaintance with Toomer's widow, Marjorie Content Toomer--and Griffin accepts her belief that Gurdjieff's influence significantly contributed to her husband's literary decline. Rich in detail and anecdote, Griffin's study concludes with his 1972 interview with Marjorie Content Toomer. A scholarly apparatus including primary sources and a number of photographs--some previously unpublished--add another dimension to Griffin's study. **Summing Up:** Recommended. Toomer scholars and specialists in African American literature; upper-division undergraduates through faculty. -- *J. A. Miller, George Washington University*
Review in 2003 Apr CHOICE

THE UNCOLLECTED WORKS OF AMERICAN AUTHOR JEAN TOOMER, 1894-1967

by John Chandler Griffin

0-7734-6810-2   440pp.   2003

This collection nicely complements Darwin Turner's *The Wayward and the Seeking: A Collection of Writings by Jean Toomer* (CH, Oct'80) and Frederik Rusch's *A Jean Toomer Reader: Selected Unpublished Writings* (CH, Oct'94) by gathering most of Toomer's published poems, short stories, plays, and essays into a single volume. Organized chronologically, from 1922 to 1950, and divided into three major sections, the material here captures several distinct stages of Toomer's career. Author of *Biography of American Author Jean Toomer, 1894-1967* (CH, Apr'03), Griffin offers a brief overview of Toomer's life and work but is content to let his carefully annotated selections speak for themselves; the result enriches understanding of Toomer's artistic and spiritual preoccupations in the decades following the critical success of *Cane* (1923). A welcome addition to Toomer scholarship, the present title will be of particular interest to Toomer specialists, but it will appeal to readers with developed interests in Toomer as well. **Summing Up:** Recommended. Upper-division undergraduates through faculty. -- *J. A. Miller, George Washington University*
Review in 2003 Sept CHOICE

DONALD BARTHELME, POSTMODERNIST AMERICAN WRITER

by Michael Thomas Hudgens

0-7734-7479-X   220pp.   2001

Hudgens (literature and philosophy, South Dakota School
of Mines & Technology) focuses on Barthelme as a postmodernist whose fiction coalesces through the employ-
ment of collages of deconstructed patterns. The book will
serve best as an introduction for the first-time serious
reader of Barthelme's fiction: it summarizes and quotes
extensively both from Barthelme's texts and from the primary canon of Barthelme criticism by such writers as
John Barth, Jerome Klinkowitz, William Gaddis, William
Gass, and Larry McCaffery. Hudgens opens the study
with major emphasis on the story "On Angels" as "a microcosm of Barthelme's creative dilemma as a Postmodern
fiction writer"; the penultimate chapter offers an analysis
of *The Dead Father* (CH, Mar'76) as "a meditation about
the world." The last chapter, primarily summary, covers
Barthelme's final publications, including the novel *Paradise* (CH, Mar'87) and "Tickets," the last of his stories to
appear in *The New Yorker* before his death in 1996.
Hudgens also makes reference to a number of other writ-
ers--William Blake, Ezra Pound, Umberto Eco, and especially James Joyce--a fact that increases the book's value
for undergraduates approaching Barthelme for the first
time. -- *W. B. Warde Jr., University of North Texas*
Review in 2002 Feb CHOICE

REDISCOVERING STEINBECK: REVISIONIST VIEWS OF HIS ART, POLITICS, AND INTELLECT

by Cliff Lewis and Carroll Britch

0-88946-169-4   277pp.   1989

Although this collection is unlikely to effect a major change in Steinbeck's reputation, most of the 12 essays included here will be of interest to students and scholars investigating the complex career of a writer whose ambition frequently exceeded his achievement. Divided into sections titled "The Artist in Process" and "The Artist in Society," the collection is most useful for the light it casts on relatively obscure Steinbeck material (his uncollected stories, speeches written for Franklin Roosevelt, and the filmscript for Viva Zapata!) and on Steinbeck's sources (Robert DeMott's excellent discussion of the 19th-century medical guide Gunn's New Family Physician in East of Eden and John Ditsky's suggestive speculation on the parallels between The Moon Is Down and the thought of Randolph Bourne). In addition, Louis Owens's reconsideration of his previous harsh judgment of the narrative voice of East of Eden and an essay documenting the misogynistic perspective of The Wayward Bus will be of interest to future scholars of those works. The only serious flaw in the collection, which would have benefited from at least some discussion of The Grapes of Wrath, is the editors' essay on Steinbeck's treatment of Indian characters, which perpetuates cultural stereotypes while seeking to justify Steinbeck's symbolic simplification of Native American characters. Levels: graduate and upper-division undergraduate. -- *C. Werner, University of Wisconsin-- Madison*
Review in 1990 May CHOICE

A COMPREHENSIVE STUDY OF AMERICAN WRITER ELIZABETH STUART PHELPS, 1844-1911: ART FOR TRUTH'S SAKE

by Ronna Coffey Privett

0-7734-6664-9   316pp.   2003

Privett (Lubbock Christian Univ.) has delivered on the promise of the title of this ambitious volume, which indeed provides a comprehensive study of Phelps. In the introduction, however, the author dwells a bit too long on the critical neglect of Phelps in recent years and takes some shots at previous critics, complaining that some studies have been "too often apologetic in tone." Once Privett has established Phelps's importance in literary history, though, she hits her stride, offering insightful and sophisticated analyses of such works as *The Story of Avis*, *The Silent Partner*, *Dr. Zay*, *The Gates Ajar*, *Beyond the Gates*, and *The Gates Between*. Throughout the text Privett weaves snippets of Phelps's autobiography that help to illuminate various themes in her writings, and she discusses the social and cultural milieu of Phelps's generation. One minor criticism: the publisher's use of double spacing throughout the edition leaves readers feeling as though they are reading a manuscript rather than a published book. The volume features a useful chronology, several well-selected photographs, a comprehensive bibliography, and an adequate, though not particularly detailed, index. **Summing Up:** Recommended. All academic libraries; all levels. -- *D. D. Knight, SUNY College at Cortland*
Review in 2004 Jan CHOICE

WILLA CATHER AND CLASSICAL MYTH: THE SEARCH FOR A NEW PARNASSUS

by Mary Ruth Ryder

0-88946-113-9   312pp.   1990

An interesting and well-focused study of the influence of classical myth on Cather's early fiction and poetry. Ryder is interested in chronicling the tension between the "Dionysian eagerness for life" and the "Apollonian devotion to pure art" that suffuses Cather's fiction. The study is most convincing in its early chapters on Cather's experience of the classics and their influence upon The Troll Garden, April Twilights, Alexander's Bridge, O Pioneers!, The Song of the Lark, and My Antonia. Ryder's work would serve as an excellent complement to Sharon O'Brien's biography, Willa Cather: The Emerging Voice (CH, Nov'87), and to Marilyn Callander's Willa Cather and the Fairy Tale (CH, May'89). Ryder is less compelling in her reading of Cather's mature novels of the late 1920s and early 1930s. In The Professor's House, Death Comes for the Archbishop, and Shadows on the Rock, Cather's profound explanation of fundamental Christian mysteries is beyond the scope of this limited but helpful study. Levels: graduate and upper-division undergraduate. -- *L. Winters, College of Saint Elizabeth*
Review in 1990 Nov CHOICE

HISTORIOGRAPHICAL TRENDS IN EARLY JAPAN

by John R. Bentley

0-7734-7246-0   240pp.   2002

At the heart of this book are first time translations of texts
that supplement and provide perspective on more standard
accounts, thereby identifying areas of contested history
and refining the understanding of the development of historical genres. Bentley (Northern Illinois Univ.) demonstrates that *Kogo shûi (shui)* , the lengthiest text presented
here, was written to document the Imibe clan's claim to
equal status with the Nakatomi as court liturgists. Done
with erudition and care, this and the other translations,
along with an initial discursive and analytic chapter, ad-
vance scholarship in the field. **Summing Up**: Optional.
Addressed primarily to specialists. -- *C. Schirokauer, Columbia University*
Review in 2003 June CHOICE

A Bibliography of the Malayan campaign and the Japanese period in West Malaysia, Singapore and Borneo, 1941-1945

by Justin Corfield

0-7734-7352-1   418pp.   2001

Corfield's bibliography exhaustively covers the WW II era in Malaya, Singapore, and Borneo through Japanese attack, occupation, and defeat. More than 4,000 items are included: books and chapters in books, official government publications, magazine and newspaper articles, dissertations and theses, book reviews, archival collections, and interviews. Arrangement is strictly alphabetical by author or other main entry; entries are numbered. Some annotations are supplied. Basic indexes for subjects, service units (British and Commonwealth military), and people (many of them authors of the works included). Best suited to Asian studies and WW II collections. -- *E. F. Konerding, Wesleyan University*
Review in 2002 June CHOICE

A Bibliography of Military and Political Aspects of the Malayan Emergency, the Confrontation with Indonesia, and the Brunei Revolt

by Justin Corfield

0-7734-6715-7   408pp.   2003

Corfield provides an extensive, helpful reference guide to books, articles, theses, and other publications, mainly in English, about the Malayan emergency (1948-60), the confrontation with Indonesia (1963-66) and the Brunei revolt (1962). Access to the more than 4,500 bibliographic citations, which are arranged by author and are unannotated, is provided by subject and personal name indexes. While coverage of English-language sources is very extensive, Corfield includes only a few citations for Dutch- or Malay-language publications, but he supplies a selected chronology on the emergency and related topics for the years 1945-89. This useful reference volume will facilitate study and research on the military history, general history, and politics of the early post-WW II era in Malaya/Malaysia, Singapore, and Brunei. A related bibliography by the same compiler (*A Bibliography of the Malayan Campaign and the Japanese Period in West Malaysia, Singapore and Borneo, 1941-1945*, CH, Jun'02) covers events of the preceding, bitterly contested, WW II years in this region. **Summing Up:** Recommended. General readers; upper-division undergraduates and higher. -- *L. S. Dutton, emeritus, Northern Illinois University*
Review in 2004 Feb CHOICE

BIBLIOGRAPHY ON
EAST ASIAN RELIGION AND PHILOSOPHY

by James T. Bretzke

0-7734-7318-1   584pp.   2001

Bretzke's book cites bibliographic and Internet resources about East Asia (mainly China, Japan, and Korea) in philosophy and religious studies. The first section treats general works on philosophy and religion in all of Asia. The second section concentrates on the major religious and philosophical traditions of East Asia--Buddhism, Confucianism, and Taoism. These sections also cite sources on Chinese and Confucian understanding of religion, business and economics ethics in Asia, human rights in East Asian contexts, and Asian women's philosophy and theology. Following these sections are geographical sections for China, Japan, and Korea, with subdivisions by religious themes. The bibliography cites a wide variety of Internet resources on East Asian art, geography, history, and culture, with lists of virtual libraries, online electronic journals, Internet discussion groups, etc. An extensive index by author and subject is provided. Faculty and professionals. -- *J. Cheng, Southern Connecticut State University*
Review in 2002 Mar CHOICE

ESSAYS, INTERVIEWS, RECOLLECTIONS AND UNPUBLISHED MATERIAL OF GU CHENG, 20TH-CENTURY CHINESE POET

by Li Xia

0-7734-8005-6   488pp.   1999

Li Xia (Univ. of Newcastle, Australia) has published other studies and translations of this enigmatic poet, influential critical essayist, and leading young intellectual from the late 1970s until his tragic death. This collection of critical essays on Gu Cheng's writings and thought, translations of interviews, and unpublished letters provides the most probing look to date into the mind and heart of this leading "misty poet." From both Chinese and Western scholars and colleagues, essays, studies, and interviews examine Gu Cheng's literary genius and the tormented soul he revealed through his poems and letters. Li Xia appends both a useful chronology of Gu Cheng's life and a comprehensive bibliography. Full of competent and interesting resources, this volume is strongly recommended for libraries that wish to go beyond basic coverage of contemporary Chinese literature. -- *J. W. Walls, Simon Fraser University*
Review in 2000 May CHOICE

Bibliography of Syrian Archaeological Sites to 1980

by Howard C. Bybee

0-7734-9040-X   248pp.   1995

More than 1,800 articles and books on Syrian archaeology written prior to 1980 are gathered in this well-organized bibliography. While a few broader archaeological bibliographies exist such as Jill Phillips's Archaeology of the Collective East (1977), this source is unique for researchers in Near East archaeology, religious studies, and history focusing on Syria, particularly since the earlier works it cites would otherwise be quite difficult to locate. Since more recent articles and books are becoming increasingly easy to access online, however, updates to the bibliography are not planned. In part 1, entries are listed by site and arranged by author then chronologically by date of publication. The articles and books listed in part 2 are broader in scope and are listed under three topical sections: "Chronique," "Prehistory," and "Survey." Part 3 lists the sources used in compiling the bibliography. Supplementing the clear-cut organization are author and heading indexes. This very useful and comprehensive listing of research and reports written in Western languages includes a few citations to articles written in Arabic. General; academic. -- *P. I. Nielson, Rand Corporation*
Review in 1996 Mar CHOICE

THE SACRED GEOGRAPHY OF THE AMERICAN MOUND BUILDERS

by Maureen Korp

0-88946-484-7   140pp.   1990

Korp argues that the earthen mounds built by Amerindians in the Mississippi and Ohio river valleys from 1500 BCE to 1200 CE were religious sites where the bodies, bones, and ashes of the dead were interred. Korp attributes the tendency to orient the mounds in an easterly direction to the wish to warm the dead by the sun as it rose in the sky. As Korp explains, the social disruptions caused by death were diminished as the dead remained present to their communities in their sun-warmed, earthen homes. Unlike many overreaching theories about prehistoric Amerindian religion, Korp's arguments are based on every point on a careful assessment of the evidence and its limits. The book includes a good selection of technical illustrations, a very useful bibliography, and an appendix arguing that the incised, pigmented stones found in the Ohio valley, known as the "Adena tablets," were used to paint the bodies of the dead with the preservative red ochre. Recommended for all libraries with collections in Native American archaeology. -- *A. Porterfield, Syracuse University*
Review in 1991 Feb CHOICE

THE LIFE AND WORK OF
THE TWENTIETH-CENTURY LOUISIANA ARCHITECT,
A. HAYS TOWN

by David H. Sachs

0-7734-6686-X   240pp.   2003

Sachs (architecture, Kansas State Univ., Manhattan) has
written this chronologically arranged story of the architec-
tural career of A. Hays Town. Town was trained at Tulane
University in the early 1920s, practiced in Mississippi
during the decade of the Great Depression with a partner
named Overstreet, and finished his career in Louisiana,
working--remarkably--into the early 1990s. Town was
trained in the beaux-arts method but accommodated himself to variations on modernism in the 1930s and 1940s,
subsequently shifting to a more comfortable southern ver-
nacular. The author briefly describes many of Town's
buildings, giving readers the sense that Town enjoyed a
long and successful career and left a legacy of good buildings, but as an eclectic never really developed a signature
style. **Summing Up:** Recommended. General readers;
professionals; two-year technical program students. -- *J.
Quinan, University at Buffalo, SUNY*
Review in 2004 Mar CHOICE

BUSINESS, COMMERCE, AND SOCIAL RESPONSIBILITY: BEYOND AGENDA

by Richard H. Reeves-Ellington and Adele Anderson

0-7734-8442-6   288pp.   1997

This reader-friendly, well-structured, and substantive book proposes a new approach to social responsibility of transnational corporations operating in multiple cultural settings. The authors, practitioner-anthropologists, argue for a "culture-based ethics" (versus an "agenda-driven ethics") to integrate business organizations with the whole of society, exemplifying their view with interesting case studies. Do they achieve their goals? Partially. They succeed in broadening the notion of pure business toward "commerce" (including an indispensable sociocultural dimension); in linking responsibility to personal agency and freedom; and in seriously discussing the sociocultural context, especially relevant to international business. However, there are also some shortcomings. Despite the authors' "basic doctrinal stance" in favor of "loyalty to business," their concept of responsibility is basically empty of content. Their criticism of the agenda-driven ethics seems to ignore the fundamental questions of ethics, which is, after all, about action. Moreover, their approach, like many others regarding "business and society," jumps from the business organization directly to the sociocultural context while overlooking the crucial fact, particularly in international business, that companies always operate within a certain economic system. Nevertheless, this is an important book. Recommended for upper-division undergraduate through professional collections. -- *G. Enderle, University of Notre Dame*
Review in 1998 June CHOICE

An Annotated Bibliography on the History of Usury and Interest from the Earliest Times Through the Eighteenth Century

by John M. Houkes

0-7734-6456-5   600pp.   2004

Houkes's extensive and remarkably readable annotated bibliography on usury and interest will appeal to a wide range of readers, not just scholars of economics and finance. Theologians, philosophers, social historians, and anthropologists, to name a few, will discover valuable citations related to their fields. Houkes presents with clarity an overview of the major literature, choosing factual presentation over interpretation and commentary. He provides full bibliographic citations and succinct, accurate summaries for every entry, as well as brief biographical information for many of the authors. English translations are given for key quotations. Chapters proceed chronologically, starting with the beginning of recorded history in Ancient Mesopotamia through the end of the 18th century. Introductory essays place each section in historical context and provide a straightforward picture of the debate on usury for each time period. Houkes notes sources of bibliographic reference, indexes names and anonymous titles, and supplies a supplementary bibliography of later important sources. Houkes excludes works in Scandinavian or Slavic languages, but this detracts little from the scope and richness of his work. **Summing Up:** Highly recommended. All libraries, especially those supporting graduate programs in finance, economics, history, or religion. -
- C. A. Ross, DePaul University
Review in 2004 Nov CHOICE

UNDERSTANDING CONTEMPORARY CUBA IN VISUAL AND VERBAL FORMS: MODERNISM REVISITED

by Max Dorsinville

0-7734-6576-6   212pp.   2004

Dorsinville (English, McGill Univ.) brings an interdisciplinary approach to contemporary Cuban studies. A photographer, he documented research trips to Havana, Santa Clara, and Matanzas with photographs and, in a process he describes as "a reconciliation of sense and thought," he combines these photographs with critical commentaries of contemporary Cuba. These personal commentaries draw from a variety of intellectual trends (particularly his readings on postcolonial theory) and his own background as a black Haitian. At the book's core is Dorsinville's treatment of a variety of texts by Christina Garcia, Edmundo Desnoes, and Antonio Benítez (Benitez) Rojo. The author incorporates in this socioethnic and political exploration of "Cubanness" discussion of three non-Cuban writers who attempted to comprehend the Cuban experience: Graham Greene, Ernest Hemingway, and Pico Iyer. This volume will be most useful to those seeking an introduction to sociopolitical issues of contemporary Cuban culture. **Summing Up:** Recommended. Lower/upper-division undergraduates and graduates students. -- *R. Ocasio, Agnes Scott College*
Review in 2004 Sept CHOICE

THE COLONIAL SUBJECT'S SEARCH FOR NATION, CULTURE, AND IDENTITY IN THE WORKS OF JULIA ÁLVAREZ, ROSARIO FERRÉ, AND ANA LYDIA VEGA

by Eda B. Henao

0-7734-6551-0   162pp.   2003

Though Henao deserves credit for her valiant attempt to look at important matters, her choice of topics is perhaps more important and successful than her handling of them. Alvarez, Ferré, and Vega need to be studied in terms of postcolonial and colonial attitudes, racial concepts and prejudices, and feminist issues, but covering all three areas is a gargantuan task and results here in some quick comparisons that lead nowhere. Conceived too broadly, terms like "nation," "culture," and "identity" can become a problem by being too abstract and diffuse to be useful. Although her book is interesting because it looks equally into Spanish- and English-language novels by women from Puerto Rico and the Dominican Republic, it will likely be hard to learn from, even for specialists. In addition to taking on several large themes and dealing with breezy definitions of her concepts, she also attributes unusual and broad meanings to some ideas, e.g., "feminine writing" (which she defines as the "presence of a feminist consciousness"). **Summing Up:** Optional. Comprehensive collections serving graduate and research collections. --
D. E. Marting, University of Mississippi
Review in 2004 July CHOICE

AN ETHNOGRAPHY OF COSMOPOLITANISM IN KINGSTON, JAMAICA

by Huon Wardle

0-7734-7552-4   256pp.   2000

This ethnographic inquiry into the social and cultural experience of poor urban dwellers in socially heterogeneous Kingston, Jamaica, describes how Kingstonians create meaningful lives for themselves in a milieu characterized by urbanization and globalization rather than a strong national culture. The author draws on the work of the Enlightenment philosopher Kant, for whom personhood was self-created rather than conveyed through tradition or culture, and of Georg Simmel, theorist of cosmopolitan society and Kant's intellectual disciple, who posited the existence of two distinct cultures: the individual's own imaginative culture and the external culture of history and tradition. Arguing that Jamaicans experience continual "tension" between their desire for a sense of place, geographically and socially, and their desire for freedom through geographical movement, the author demonstrates how they simultaneously develop satisfying social networks and create meaning for themselves within the wider frameworks of cosmopolitanism and "deterritorialism" that govern their lives. Personal narratives and fieldwork diary excerpts enliven the book's otherwise dense academic prose. For advanced students and professionals familiar with basic tenets of social and cultural anthropology, philosophy, and social theory. -- *M. A. Gwynne, SUNY at Stony Brook*
Review in 2001 May CHOICE

THE PYTHAGOREAN INTERTEXT IN OVID'S METAMORPHOSES: A NEW INTERPRETATION

by Maria Maddalena Colavito

0-88946-398-0   164pp.   1989

Critics have always found the Pythagorean episode a
stumbling block, considering it either a tedious bore, one
of the poet's typical playful jokes, or an unconvincing attempt to give his theme a philosophical basis. Colavito
suggests that the Metamorphoses is a neo-Pythagorean
text and that the carmen and error which occasioned the
poet's exile may not have been the Ars Amatoria but the
Metamorposes itself and the error the poet's affiliation
with a Neo-Pythagorean sect. Interpreting the theme of
transformations as "internally Pythagorean," she demonstrates that the Pythagorean belief in number as the origin
of the ordering of the cosmos can be seen throughout.
This connection is clearly set forth in the initial account of
the four elements that the demiurge successfully combines
and subdivides, thus conforming to the Pythagorean tet-
ractys, "the symbolic key to all creation...beginning with
the one' and ending with four'." Metamorphosis, metapsy-
chosis, and transmigration constitute a fundamental tenet
of Pythagoreanism. Seven pertinent appendixes (e.g., Pythagorean sources and music, the Emerald Stone, a table
of transformations and translations of selected Ovidian
passages) and a comprehensive bibliography complete the
book. The continuing popularity and influence of the
poem through the ages and diverse attempts to solve the
enigma of the poet's purpose make further investigations
always important. This book is a challenge to the thoughtful reader. -- *B. N. Quinn, Mount Holyoke College*
Review in 1990 Mar CHOICE

BIBLIOGRAPHY OF THE MYTH OF DON JUAN IN LITERARY HISTORY

Edited by José Manuel Losada

0-7734-8450-7   236pp.   1997

Losada's bibliography differs significantly from that of Armand Singer, whose 40 years of research culminated in 1993 with *The Don Juan Theme: An Annotated Bibliography of Version, Analogues, Uses and Adaptations* (CH, Mar'94). Singer cast his net widely, including other seducers (Casanova, Lovelace) and noting numerous allusions or comparisons to Don Juan. Losada and his colleagues include only works that use the name Don Juan in one form or another (Don Juan, Don Giovanni, Don Zhuan) and that substantially incorporate the entire myth, including an inquiry into transcendence, the presence of a group of women, a banquet or feast, and the threat of a deadline. Unlike Singer, Losada includes translations and major editions. In addition, critical studies were omitted from Singer's 1993 edition but comprise 1,708 of Losada's 2,884 entries. The entries are divided by language into English, French, German, Italian, Portuguese, and Spanish, with an appendix on the Slavonic languages. The index cross-references all the criticism pertaining to major authors. More languages and more extensive indexing are promised in future editions. Singer's inclusiveness has its rewards, but students focusing on major treatments of the myth will find more help in Losada. -- *B. E. Brandt, South Dakota State University*
Review in 1998 Mar CHOICE

The Romantic and Transcendental Quests of Ralph Waldo Emerson and Victor-Marie Hugo

by Regina M. Young

0-7734-6668-1   494pp.   2003

Like many other volumes in the "Studies in Comparative Literature" series, the subject of this one appears at first glance strained or irrelevant. As Young (Univ. of Missouri, Rolla) documents, Emerson and Hugo never met though their paths came close to intersecting a number of times. And although they both knew of each other, they seem not to have read much--if anything--of each others' works. Temperamentally they were very different men. Hugo was passionate and spontaneous whereas Emerson was temperate and restrained. These and other disparities that separate the two men appear greater than anything they might have held in common. Thus, the prospective reader's question might be, "What is the value of a comparative study of these two?" The answer lies in the spirit of 19th-century transcendental Romanticism that the two shared and voiced in their own ways. As Young makes clear, independence of thought and spirit, a desire for personal and social freedom, and a love of nature with a tendency toward pantheism are among the characteristics that echo within the writings of both Emerson and Hugo. **Summing Up:** Optional. Graduate and research collections. -- *P. J. Ferlazzo, Northern Arizona University* **Review in 2004 May CHOICE**

A History of Dance in American Higher Education: Dance and the American University

by Thomas K. Hagood

0-7734-7799-3   428pp.   2000

Hagood (Mills College) traces historical influences on the development of dance studies in academia. The significance of early dance programs such as those at Wisconsin, Bennington, and the Federal Theater Project is interestingly described. Generously acknowledging the vision of leaders like Alma Hawkins, Hagood traces the history of dance organizations such as NDA and CODA and also astutely discusses cultural influences on dance in academia including the "dance bust" during the 1980s. Topics such as strategies for survival, anti-intellectualism in dance, and schisms between practitioners and academics in the arts are covered here. An early chapter discusses dance writings from 1930 to 1940 as the beginnings of "dance as an intellectual activity." Hagood concludes by acknowledging the influences on current dance writing and scholarship of hot topics like technology and multiculturalism. Hagood suggests that a broader curriculum leads not only to difficulties but also to new avenues for scholarship and ultimately to new programs that reflect the current society. An astute history of the integration of dance into colleges and universities, this volume will interest all students of dance and should be required reading for anyone aspiring to teach dance in academia. -- *J. Friesen, emeritus, University of Houston*
Review in 2000 Dec CHOICE

AGRIPPINOVA VAGANOVA (1879-1951): HER PLACE IN THE HISTORY OF BALLET AND HER IMPACT ON THE FUTURE OF CLASSICAL DANCE

by Peggy Willias-Aarnio

0-7734-7074-3   696pp.   2002

Vaganova technique is one of the few codified ballet techniques in existence. Willis-Aarnio (Texas Tech Univ.) dis-
covered Vaganova's pedagogy in the early 1970s and since
then has worked hard to preserve and transmit the teaching
method. With the publication of this massive book, the ballet world finally has a scholarly work describing the teaching method. The author looks at how Vaganova took huge
amounts of information, distilled it to its essence, and then
organized the material into a rational method that could be
consistently and accurately taught. Willis-Aarnio also captures the passion characteristic of the Russian people. She
provides Russian documentation, translated into English
for the first time, showing some of the connections between many of the significant people in the world of dance
at that time. From Pavlova, Nijinsky, and Balanchine, who
were members of the Imperial Theatre during Vaganova's
performing career, to Ulanova, who was one of her pupils,
Vaganova's influence can be easily seen and felt. This reviewer found the appendixes especially illuminating--e.g.,
"Ballet Timeline" and "Classical Ballet Lineage." **Summing Up:** Highly recommended. All collections supporting
the study and performance of classical ballet. -- *L. K.
Rosenberg, Miami University*
Review in 2003 July CHOICE

THE MOVEMENT FOR COMMUNITY CONTROL OF NEW YORK CITY'S SCHOOLS, 1966-1970: CLASS WARS
by Derek Edgell

(Jointly reviewed with "The Moderates' Dilemma" by M.D. Lassiter & A. B. Lewis)

0-7734-8262-8   532pp.   1998

These two books offer unique perspectives on the problems surrounding racial integration of schools. In 1956, the Virginia General Assembly passed a package of massive resistance laws removing authority for pupil transfers from local boards and cutting off state funding to any local school system that desegregated. In 1959, the Virginia Supreme Court and a panel of federal judges invalidated these laws. Lassiter (Bowdoin College) and Lewis (Univ. of Virginia) present a collection of six essays, many from a seminar at the University of Virginia, describing how moderate white residents of Virginia reacted. For example, the first essay describes how Armistead Lloyd Boothe, elected by the political organization of Harry Byrd Sr. to the Virginia legislature, sought reform, reluctantly voted for the massive resistance laws, and finally parted from the machine. Another essay analyzes how James J. Kilpatrick, then editor of the *Richmond News Leader*, popularized the theory of interposition, making resistance to the US Supreme Court appear legal. The third essay tells how nine white women in Charlottesville opposed the segregationists' willingness to sacrifice public schooling by offering the temporary alternative of emergency schooling.

Unlike Virginia, New York officially opposed segregation. Yet, the residential areas of Harlem, the South Bronx, and central-eastern Brooklyn comprised the largest concentration of African Americans in the US. The population included angry black militants, many conservative African Americans from a range of social classes, and the remnants of a once large white population, mostly Jewish. By 1965, black leaders of multiracial organizations that had fought for integration, such as the Congress for Racial Equality (CORE), embraced separatist ideals in Brooklyn, driving out many Jewish members. In 1967, New York schools began demonstration projects in such areas as Ocean Hill-Brownsville, and different elements in the community clashed. From his detailed and complex account, Edgell (Univ. of Southampton New College, England) determines that community control could be seen as a radical policy that offered the opportunity for community-wide change. However, he notes that it could be conservative because, at best, it allowed the residents to run their own ghettos without resources or direction for improvement. Readers who want to know more about the racial desegregation of schools, the motivation behind massive resistance, and community control should also consult Jennifer L. Hochschild's *The New American Dilemma: Liberal Democracy and School Desegregation* (CH, Mar'85). All levels. -- *J. Watras, University of Dayton*
Review in 1999 May CHOICE

A HISTORY OF THE FLEET PRISON, LONDON: THE ANATOMY OF THE FLEET

by Roger Lee Brown

0-7734-8762-X   372pp.   1996

The Fleet, London's prison for debtors, can be traced to 1189, but its notoriety dates from the later 17th century to its 1842 dissolution. Debtors were not criminals and thus not there for punishment. The warden bore the costs (and profits) of keeping the prisoners. This combination meant debtors of means lived well: they were allowed out for the day so long as they or their families could afford to pay the keeper that accompanied them. They could rent the best rooms, share them with their families, and treat the Fleet as a sanctuary from their creditors. Those without means lived a meager existence and were often the objects of charity. Statistics reveal prisoners from every social class; most had the means to live above the charity line (there were alternate, less desirable prisons for destitute debtors). More than 80 percent were there for less than three years, reaching accommodation with their creditors or availing themselves of Parliament's frequent insolvency acts. Brown's sources--legal disputes between warden and prisoners, parliamentary inquiries, and literary accounts-- emphasize problems and scandal, but if the warden could maintain a prison of more than 300 debtors with only five employees, tensions cannot have been very great. Upper-division undergraduates and above. -- *J. W. Weingart, Whitman College*
Review in 1997 Apr CHOICE

THE SCOTTISH REGENCY OF THE EARL OF ARRAN: A STUDY IN THE FAILURE OF ANGLO-SCOTTISH RELATIONS

by David Franklin

0-7734-8971-1   228pp.   1995

Franklin's study of Anglo-Scottish relations, 1543-1554, investigates the regency of James Hamilton, second Earl of Arran. Arran, one of the "little men in Scotland," as Franklin describes him, confronted the menacing schemes of Henry VIII to subvert Scottish sovereignty through treaty and marriage alliance, and when that failed, through the "rough wooing" of war. Arran's pro-English sympathies, particularly in religion, and his unimpressive character have misled his contemporaries, both Scottish and English, as well as most historians, regarding his achievements. Henry VIII saw Arran as the ideal instrument to bring about the "natural union" of two Protestant kingdoms with shared interests. Franklin (Young Harris College) argues that Arran's reluctance to confront his critics and enemies at home and in England, and his prolonged temporizing have obscured an essentially nationalist position that led to the revival of the Auld Alliance with France and preserved Scottish independence in a decade of great peril. Based almost entirely on printed sources, this well-crafted study of a critical episode in the military-diplomatic history of England and Scotland will be of interest to upper-division undergraduates and above. -- *C. W. Wood Jr., Western Carolina University*
Review in 1996 Jan CHOICE

GEORGE ELIOT AND VICTORIAN ATTITUDES TO RACIAL DIVERSITY, COLONIALISM, DARWINISM, CLASS, GENDER, AND JEWISH CULTURE AND PROPHECY

by Brenda McKay

0-7734-6621-5   604pp.   2003

In this painstakingly researched and broadly focused study, McKay takes pains to depict George Eliot as a believer in what is now called "multiculturalism." The author works hard to defend Eliot from detractors like Edward Said, who saw her as an "orientalist" complicit with European colonialism, and McKay's struggle to make George Eliot seem like an intellectual who would be at home in any contemporary English setting colors the entire book. At one point McKay even defends Eliot's investments: she purchased Indian railway shares, and McKay admits that Eliot had "no dislike of money," a serious charge indeed! Despite the unnecessary special pleading, McKay has much to say about Victorian attitudes toward "race" (which, in that era, included Judaism) and class and the relationship between those issues and Darwinism and colonialism. Her focus leads her to lean heavily on less-known works in the Eliot canon--e.g., *Theophrastus Such* and her dramatic poem "The Spanish Gipsy"--but she offers useful readings of major works, including *Felix Holt* and *Middlemarch*; her extended discussion and analysis of *Daniel Deronda* is excellent. Extensive notes and bibliography. **Summing Up:** Recommended. Graduate students, researchers, faculty. -- *S. F. Klepetar, St. Cloud State University*
Review in 2004 May CHOICE

BISHOP BECK AND ENGLISH EDUCATION, 1949-1959

by Francis R. Phillips

0-88946-796-X   304pp.   1990

A highly specialized study of the efforts of Bishop George
Andrew Beck and the English Catholic church to amend
the comprehensive Education Act of 1944. Provisions of
this act placed a heavier financial burden than previously
on religious groups that maintained their own schools.
Beck led the successful political struggle to change these
provisions that resulted in the Education Bill of 1959. The
author provides a judicious treatment of Bishop Beck.
Those especially interested in questions of church-state
relations will find this work valuable, but only specialized
libraries will want it in their holdings. -- *S. Fishman, University
of Wisconsin--Madison*
Review in 1990 Dec CHOICE

REPRESENTING RAPE IN THE ENGLISH EARLY MODERN PERIOD

by Barbara J. Baines

0-7734-6861-7   324pp.   2003

Baines (North Carolina State Univ.) has written an enlightening and much-needed interdisciplinary study of rape in Renaissance literature. Placing her literary study contextually within the legal system and politics of the Jacobean court, the author frames her discussion of the literature by examining three relatively obscure Old Testament accounts of rape and Renaissance theological commentary on the texts (her first chapter) and Renaissance visual depictions of rapes (her last). Her discussion of "literary" rape encompasses Shakespeare's *Rape of Lucrece*, Marlowe's *Hero and Leander*, Nashe's *Unfortunate Traveller*, and (briefly) Gascoigne's *Adventures of Master F.J.* Later chapters show that contemporary popular stage plays "reflect and produce the gender ideology of the period." Baines's volume compares favorably with the growing number of studies (for example, Chris Mounsey's and Ian Frederick Moulton's) on pornography and general lewdness in early modern culture--although Baines concentrates on the most brutal and most basic kind of sexual aggression in early modern literature and culture. This reviewer was disappointed not to find a discussion of Milton's *Comus*, but Baines's excellent discussion of Shakespeare's *Rape* more than made up for the omission. **Summing Up:** Highly recommended. Upper-division undergraduates through researchers and faculty. -- *D. Aldrich-Watson, University of Missouri--St. Louis*
Review in 2003 Sept CHOICE

LITERATURE, CULTURE, AND SOCIETY IN POSTWAR ENGLAND, 1945-1965

by John Brannigan

0-7734-7169-3   320pp.   2002

Branningan's premise is that the traditional focus of literary criticism on the so-called movement poets and the "angry young men" must be supplemented by attention to a less-known group of writers whose subjects were the problems of working class life, the exploitation of women, the marginalization of homosexuals, and the impact of immigration on English society. Those writing in this vein contested the conservative postwar political and cultural consensus, and their presence contradicts the claim that postwar English literature "failed" to speak to the condition of the times or to imagine an England with alternative futures. Brannigan extends Alan Sinfield's *Literature, Politics, and Culture in Postwar Britain* (1989; 2nd ed., 1997) and enlarges the literary terrain through analyses of important works by Nell Dunn, John Petty, Samuel Selvon, Rose Macauley, and others. He focuses on the writers and their characters' contentious engagement with a society in transition, struggling against its conservatism and revealing new voices and new experience. The final two chapters on postcolonial (immigrant) writings and the *English* West Indian renaissance provide substantial and insightful treatment of "the voice of the periphery" speaking through "the language of the center" and thus exemplifying a new hybridity. Highly recommended for upper-division undergraduates and above. -- *D. Murdoch, Rochester Institute of Technology*
Review in 2002 Nov CHOICE

THE LIFE AND WORKS OF THE LANCASHIRE NOVELIST WILLIAM HARRISON AINSWORTH, 1805-1882

by Stephen James Carver

0-7734-6633-9   490pp.   2003

Hugely popular with novel readers of the 1830s and 1840s and on familiar terms with a legion of contemporaneous authors--including Charles Lamb, Leigh Hunt, Walter Scott, Bulwer-Lytton, Thackeray, Dickens, Forster-- Ainsworth has been strangely neglected by literary critics since his death. This study is almost certain to become the definitive source for his work for several reasons: it includes a complete bibliography of Ainsworth's work; a full-scale bibliography of the secondary literature; and, most important, a bibliography of his contributions to periodical literature, which were extensive and, as Carver (Univ. of East Anglia, UK) observes, deserve another book. The author has made substantial use of much previously unpublished correspondence and offers critical comment on the novels themselves, and their reception. He also suggests that books are still needed on Ainsworth's relationship to European authors of historical romance such as Alexandre Dumas, and his influence on sensation novels of the 1860s. Well written and clearly organized, this volume goes a long way toward restoring Ainsworth's place in English letters and the history of the novel. **Summing Up:** Highly recommended. Upper-division undergraduates through faculty. *-- R. T. Van Arsdel, emeritus, University of Puget Sound*
Review in 2004 Feb CHOICE

CRITICAL ESSAYS ON RONALD FIRBANK, ENGLISH NOVELIST, 1886-1926

Edited by Gill Davies, David Malcolm, and John Simons

0-7734-6555-3   236pp.   2004

Firbank (1886-1926) is a cult novelist--revered by a coterie of fans, but otherwise little known. The recent interest in gay writers has resulted in renewed interest in Firbank, and British novelist Alan Hollinghurst in particular has championed him. Since the only major book devoted to the author in the last decade is Stephen Moore's *Ronald Firbank: An Annotated Bibliography of Secondary Materials, 1905-1995* (1996), the present volume is timely. Though coeditor Simons (Edge Hill College, UK) states in his preface that the essays are "intended to stimulate interest in Firbank," readers should have a grounding in Firbank's work to get the most out of this book. For instance, Kurt Bullock's essay "Fairy Tale Fissures: The Reciprocal Quest in *Odette D'Antrevernes*" closely reads an early Firbank story, decrying the dismissal even Firbank's fans have given it. Two other critics discuss *The Flower beneath the Foot*, and the rest discuss Firbank's work collectively. This book indicates Firbank's continued influence, especially on gay readers. **Summing Up:** Recommended. Academic libraries supporting British modernism or gay studies at the upper-division undergraduate level and above; large public libraries. -- *M. J. Emery, Cottey College*
Review in 2004 Oct CHOICE

VIRGINIA WOOLF'S EXPERIMENTS WITH CONSCIOUSNESS, TIME, AND SOCIAL VALUES

by Marjorie H. Hellerstein

0-7734-7421-8   142pp.   2001

Hellerstein (emer., Massachusetts College of Art) provides a reading of Woolf's works that explores her integration of outer and inner reality; her experimentation with genre; and her insistence that form and thought are inseparable. Recognizing that Woolf saw herself as a poet, Hellerstein emphasizes the dramatic and lyrical development in Woolf's fiction and Woolf's kinship with Roger Fry in creating rather than imitating new forms. In part 1, the author explores all fiction following *The Voyage Out* and *Night and Day* (including short stories, *Jacob's Room*, *Mrs. Dalloway*, *To the Lighthouse*, *The Waves*, *Between the Acts*), reflecting Woolf's fiction as "poetic visualizations" and emphasizing the postimpressionistic desire to minimize representation. In part 2 Hellerstein reads *Orlando*, *Flush*, and *Freshwater* as parody, suggesting that Woolf repressed condemnation of social conventions but did not mask her anger in *A Room of One's Own* and *Three Guineas*. In the final chapter, Hellerstein brings Nathalie Sarraute into the discussion, presenting her as a novelist who explores consciousness and form in ways Woolf did. Recommended for upper-division undergraduate and graduate students, the book will also be valuable for faculty teaching Woolf. -- *N. Allen, Villanova University*

Review in 2002 May CHOICE

A BIBLIOGRAPHY OF THE ENGLISH NOVEL FROM THE RESTORATION TO THE FRENCH REVOLUTION: A CHECKLIST OF SOURCES AND CRITICAL MATERIALS, WITH PARTICULAR REFERENCE TO THE PERIOD 1660 TO 1740

by Robert I. Letellier

0-7734-1280-8   428pp.   1995

Letellier makes an honorable and decent effort to continue and extend to 1740 the bibliographic achievement of James Harner's English Renaissance Prose Fiction, 1500-1660 (CH, Jun'79). As the compiler acknowledges, this should be considered a "preliminary attempt." The period covered includes the Restoration and covers two highly influential writers, John Bunyan and Daniel Defoe. Appropriately, each is treated in a separate section placed just before an alphabetical list of individual authors, including influential novelists (e.g., Cervantes) translated into English during this period. A section of miscellaneous works includes types of fiction, American fiction, and women's studies. There is a thematic index and an index of scholars. Anonymous works are included by title. Entries for each author list individual works, then critical, but not biographical, studies. The lack of biographies may have been a mistake and has resulted in at least one notable omission, Angeline Goreau's pioneering feminist study of Aphra Behn, Reconstructing Aphra (CH, Dec'80). Even in a "preliminary" version, this work will be highly valuable for advanced research in English literature and should be available in any university or major public library supporting humanities research. It seems likely to join that select list of bibliographies known to librarians by the name or names of the compiler. -- *R. S. Bravard, Lock Haven University of Pennsylvania*
Review in 1995 Nov CHOICE

JOHN LEHMANN'S NEW WRITING: AN AUTHOR-INDEX, 1936-1950

Compiled by Ella Whitehead
With an introductory essay by John Whitehead

0-88946-384-0   120pp.   1990

John Lehmann was a partner in Leonard and Virginia Woolf's Hogarth Press during the 1930s and '40s. In 1936 he founded and edited the literary magazine known as New Writing, which continued under various titles until 1950. The contributors included many of the prominent writers of those years, such as George Orwell, V.S. Pritchett, Elizabeth Bowen, E.M. Forster, Christopher Isherwood, W.H. Auden, and Virginia Woolf. In addition, Lehmann attempted to provide a forum for working-class authors and various European writers of the political left. This index covers the eight numbers of the two series of New Writing, and all the numbers of its successor titles: Folios of New Writing, Daylight, New Writing and Daylight, and The Penguin New Writing. It is divided into four parts: poetry and drama; fiction and reportage; essays, articles and biography; and translators. John Whitehead's introductory essay describes Lehmann's career and the progress of New Writing. A list of abbreviations is included in the preface. There is an author checklist at the end of the volume. Recommended for academic collections where there is a strong interest in 20th-century British literature. -- *J. G. Packer, Central Connecticut State University*
Review in 1990 Nov CHOICE

THE MODERNIST POETICS AND EXPERIMENTAL FILM PRACTICE OF MAYA DEREN (1917-1961)

by Renata Jackson

0-7734-7147-2   252pp.   2002

According to its preface, this volume is the "first English language monograph on the work of this legendary film-maker, theorist, organizer, and activist." Basing her study on primary sources, Jackson (North Carolina School of the Arts) provides insights into the active life, aesthetic theories, and film practices of a gifted artist. The author insists that Deren belongs in the ranks of modernist film theorists; she suggests several reasons for the "relative avoidance of Deren's theoretical writings" in canonical academic texts, one being that Deren's work lacks feminist application, at least in terms familiar to feminist film theorists of the 1970s and 1980s. Jackson focuses much attention on Deren's most important theoretical work, *An Anagram of Ideas on Art, Form and Film* (1946), which has been reissued in a number of books, including *Maya Deren and the American Avant-Garde*, ed. by Bill Nichols (CH, May'02). She then considers Deren's ritualist aesthetics, her modernist film poetics, and her actual practice in filmmaking. Jackson's approach is detailed, stimulating, and enthusiastic. Deren's growing reputation as a film theorist is well served by this book. A filmography and a very helpful bibliography are included. -- *R. D. Sears, Berea College*
Review in 2003 Feb CHOICE

NAPOLEONIC IMPERIALISM AND THE SAVOYARD MONARCHY, 1773-1821: STATE BUILDING IN PIEDMONT

by Michael Broers

0-7734-8609-7   596pp.   1997

Based on a doctoral thesis, this exemplary work focuses on the impact of the "epoca francese" (French Revolution, Napoleonic, and post-Napoleonic periods) on the Piedmontese state. Broers provides a detailed examination of the main political, social, and economic trends that prevailed from 1687 to 1848, as well as a perceptive interpretation of historiography. The legacy of Napoleonic rule on the Savoyard state cannot be minimized. The French affected the municipalities and the provincial elite (propertied classes). A major political policy goal was the restoration of political and civil order in Piedmont. The French obtained stability by repressing Piedmontese resistance to indirect taxation, conscription, smuggling, and particularly, by uprooting banditry. Internal order was maintained after the fall of French hegemony in 1814. The administration of justice (Napoleonic legal system) was another legacy inherited by the Piedmontese. Persons, property, and civil rights were protected. Broers does a creditable job in juxtaposing the "epoca francese" with Piedmont, which was essentially an Italian state. Upper-division undergraduates and above. -- *C. A. Gliozzo, Michigan State University*
Review in 1997 Nov CHOICE

NEO-LAMARCKISM AND THE EVOLUTION CONTROVERSY IN FRANCE, 1870-1920

by Stuart M. Persell

0-7734-8275-X   300pp.   1999

Persell focuses on the development of neo-Lamarckism in France after 1870, and why France--deeply wounded by its resounding defeat in the Franco-Prussian war-- welcomed the move away from Darwinian evolution. The author separates the ideas of French neo-Lamarckians from the theories of Jean Baptiste Lamarck and American neo-Lamarckians, who accepted divine purpose as a part of their evolutionary scheme. The French school regarded Lamarck as the founder of evolution, retaining belief in the inheritance of acquired characteristics; however, they incorporated natural selection into their materialist and progressivist scheme, encouraged by Darwin's gradual acceptance of some environmentalist ideas in successive editions of the *Origin*. Persell strikes a balance between those modern biologists whose interpretation of post-Darwinian evolution has been called "whiggish" and those who claim the popularity of Darwinian evolution declined precipitously after Darwin's death and had little influence for the rest of the 19th century; e.g., he maintains that August Weismann's work played a critical role in shaping biology. The book promises to be useful for upper-division undergraduate and graduate students through research scholars in the biological sciences as well as those investigating the development of scientific ideas. -- *J. S. Schwartz, CUNY College of Staten Island*
Review in 1999 Sept CHOICE

Sixteenth Century French Women Writers: Marguerite d'Angoulême, Anne de Graville, the Lyonnese School, Jeanne de Jussie, Marie Dentière, Camille de Morel

by Ingrid Åkerlund

0-7734-6666-5   204pp.   2003

Another in the growing body of works presenting women writers of the French Renaissance, this volume could have been subtitled, according to Åkerlund , "Some Sixteenth Century Women Writers with Connections to Marguerite D'Angloulême." The author justifies this as follows: "By her position as a royal person she was able to inspire and help those who needed her support." However, in some cases, these connections are rather tenuous. Åkerlund begins with an extended chapter on Marguerite herself, which adds little to what is generally known of her. She then passes to other writers, specifically those mentioned in the subtitle. What is interesting is that in the chapter on the women from Lyon, the author does not limit herself to the best known. Instead, after discussing those, she goes on to treat a total of 18 other women. There is also an addendum to the last chapter concerning Hélisenne de Crenne, Nicole Estienne, and Marie de Romieu. Most of the material was presented in conference papers. There are extensive bibliographies for each chapter and a general one at the end. **Summing Up:** Optional. Upper-division undergraduate and graduate collections. -- *C. E. Campbell, Cottey College*
Review in 2004 Feb CHOICE

Strategies of "Writing the Self" in the French Modern Novel: C'est Moi, Je Crois

by Eileen M. Angelini

0-7734-7317-3   172pp.   2001

Drawing on Philippe Lejeune's theoretical work on autobiography and on narratological work by Gérard (Gerard) Genette and Dorrit Cohn (especially the latter's *Transparent Minds: Narrative Modes for Presenting Consciousness in Fiction*, CH, Mar'79), Angelini (Philadelphia Univ.) investigates the creation of autobiography through fictional modes of writing in three of the most important modern French writers of the past century. Dealing with Nathalie Sarraute's *Enfance*, Marguerite Duras's *L'Amant*, and the trilogy of fictional autobiographies that Alain Robbe-Grillet grouped as "Romanesques," the author offers a lucid analysis of the narrative structures by which these authors narrate their lives in an "autobiographical space" that is neither quite autobiography nor quite fiction. She shows how Sarraute engages in a self-dialogue that continues the exploration of the "tropisms" or psychological movements that she portrayed in her earlier fictions. The best-selling *L'Amant* also turns on narrative voices, in the first and in the third person, to enact the drama of the author's childhood spent in Indochina. And Robbe-Grillet mixes autobiography, metacommentary, and fantastic narrative projections to create his vision of himself. Recommended for those studying French literature, autobiography, or modern French fiction at the upper-division undergraduate level and above. -- *A. Thiher, University of Missouri--Columbia*
Review in 2002 Feb CHOICE

LESBIAN DESIRE IN POST-1968 FRENCH LITERATURE

by Lucille Cairns

0-7734-7110-3   504pp.   2002

Cairns (Univ. of Sterling, Scotland) examines "female-authored representations of lesbianism in French litera-ture," and more specifically realist literature. This exciting addition to the still-limited corpus of criticism on lesbian writing in French literature follows Jennifer Waelti-Walters' *Damned Women: Lesbians in French Novels, 1796-1996*, 2000). Cairns's focus on post-1968 literature allows for a detailed analysis of the texts she examines. She stresses the cultural erasing of lesbians and lesbian writers in French society and argues convincingly for the importance of including the social and cultural context in the analysis of this body of literature. As Cairns states, this extensive reading "provide[s] a useful, quasi-encyclopaedic reference tool within a hitherto unsketched mapping of post-68 French texts treating intra-female love and desire in realist mode." The organization of the vol-ume, chronologically and then alphabetically within this order, allows for an easy reading of her references and comments. Indispensable for upper-division undergradu-ate, graduate, and research collections supporting work in French literature, gender studies, and cultural studies. *-- J. Ricouart, George Mason University*
Review in 2003 Jan CHOICE

THE RECEPTION AND TRANSMISSION OF THE WORKS OF MARIE DE FRANCE, 1774-1974

Edited by Chantal Maréchal

0-7734-6599-5   360pp.   2003

An *hommage* to noted French scholar Emanuel Mickel,
this tome is an impressive, largely bio-bibliographical and
historiographical work. Author of *In Quest of Marie de
France* (1992), Maréchal (Virginia Commonwealth Univ.)
divides the material collected here into two principle parts,
"Reception" (18th to 20th centuries) and "Transmission."
Most names evoked will be familiar to students of this
material--Gaston Paris ("outed" by R.H. Bloch), Joseph
Bédier (Marie as surrealist), Hoepffner (a Renaissance
idealist for Mickel), Leo Spitzer (a methodological inno-
vator for J.R. Rothschild), and Sidney Painter (his 1933
note on Marie's patrons amplified by J.H. McCash). The
"Transmission" section touches on issues of translation (J.
Ferrante) and various textual editions, especially French
(Y. de Pontfarcy and G. Eckard). Impressive in breadth,
the volume ranges from Jambeck's 60-page account of the
English and French Enlightenment discovery of Marie to
interesting surveys by M.B. Speer, H.R. Runte, and G.S.
Burgess of 18th-, 19th-, and 20th-century editions of
Marie's modest oeuvre, which comprised three principal
texts--*Lais*, *Fables*, and *Saint Patrick's Purgatory*. **Sum-
ming Up:** Recommended. Graduate student, researchers,
faculty. -- *R. Cormier, Longwood University*
Review in 2004 May CHOICE

INTERPRETATIONS OF RABELAIS

by John Parkin

0-7734-7081-6   232pp.   2002

In this follow-up to his *Interpreting Rabelais: An Open Text Reading of an Open Text* (1993), Parkin (Bristol Univ., UK) considers the following topics: Rabelais and Guillaume Coquillart and their presentations of trials; Pantagruel's early years (his birth, education, and meeting up with Panurge); the two wars (Dipsodian and Picrocholine) compared; Pantagruel's later years (his role in Rabelais' *Le Tiers Livre* and *Le Quart Livre*, where Pantagruel states, "These are books where he has fulfilled his destiny and is in the curious position of having a literary identity which depends on his companion Panurge. . ."); the question of interpreting Bakhtin; and *Le Cinquiesme Livre*. On this last topic, Parkin tackles the question of authenticity by asking, "Can we read the *Cinquieme Livre* as in any way relevant to Rabelais' work...?" Although he never takes a stand on this thorny question, Parkin does present some interesting theories, as he does in each of the topics covered. This study may leave some with many unanswered questions, but it is a valuable addition to Rabelais scholarship. However, Parkin's polysyllabic vocabulary will baffle the casual reader, so this volume is recommended for graduate and research collections only. -- *C. E. Campbell, Cottey College*
Review in 2003 Jan CHOICE

FLORENTIN: A NOVEL

by Dorothea Mendelssohn Veit Schlegel

Translated by Edwina Lawler and Ruth Richardson

0-88946-365-4   350pp.   1989

The first English translation of a neglected novel of early
Romanticism by the wife of Friedrich Schlegel, and the
first volume of a new edition of the works of this unusual
woman. Six volumes of her correspondence, a bibliography with index, short fiction, essays, and fragments are
planned. Florentin is preceded by an introduction of indif-
ferent quality, which includes a short life of Dorothea's
father, Moses Mendelssohn, and many other standard features, such as a partial biography, contemporary and critical opinion (quoted at excessive length), a bibliography,
speculation about the model(s) for the title character, and
a catalog of the novel's typcial Romantic features. There is
some verbatim repetition in separate parts of the introduction, whose style is not always felicitous. Print reproduction is sometimes uneven to the point of illegibility. The
novel itself is competently translated, with a few awkward
renderings of German idioms and typographical errors but
with a good feeling for the poetry included at intervals in
the text. It is an exciting addition to the sources available
to English-speaking readers, and certainly unjustifiably
neglected. It has striking features: wonderful characters,
typical descriptive passages, good (though predictable)
narrative technique, much romantically unresolved mystery, and daring novelties (e.g., an abortion; scathing criticism of religion). Although future volumes may surpass
this one in scholarly preface and mechanical reproduction,
it will be difficult to imagine a more delightful discovery
than Florentin, who is so typically the brooding and
searching hero of Romantic melancholy. For all libraries.
-- *E. Glass, Rosemont College*
Review in 1989 Oct CHOICE

A STUDY OF B. TRAVEN'S FICTION: THE JOURNEY TO SOLIPAZ

by Richard E. Mezo

0-7734-9838-9   212pp.   1993

Of the many writings to appear about Traven over the years, Mezo's book-length study is the first since the 1970s to sidestep completely the thorny issue of Traven's identity and demonstrate convincingly that he had well-defined aesthetic theories, which he fully developed in certain works that, for Mezo, are masterpieces: the short stories, The Death Ship, The Cotton-Pickers, The Treasure of the Sierra Madre, and The Bridge in the Jungle. On the merits of the so-called "Jungle Novels," Mezo may be less convincing, but his attempt to rescue them from undeserved oblivion is praiseworthy. In the major works he shows that Traven borrowed motifs from Dante and Shakespeare and that his protagonists are victims of a mechanistic society where "explanations and analyses" are emphasized over human concerns. He integrates these ideas with the less successful visionary and utopian writings, in which Traven juxtaposed the simpler life of the Indian to that of the Westerner's alienation from the natural world. Highly recommended. Undergraduate; graduate; faculty. -- *H. D. Dickerson, Georgia State University*
Review in 1994 June CHOICE

Manuel Fraga Iribarne and The Rebirth of Spanish conservatism, 1939-1990

by John Gilmour

0-7734-8029-3   360pp.   1999

This is a straightforward descriptive account of the political career of Manuel Fraga Iribarne, the doyen of "respectable" Spanish conservatism from his participation in the later years of the Franco regime to his role in the transition to democracy, failed attempts to create a victorious coalition/party on the right, and finally, personal victories in his native Galicia. Still on the scene, Fraga emerges clearly as one of the most important Spanish political figures of the last 50 years and richly deserves the attention the author gives him. Although frequently controversial, his behavior and policies ultimately have benefited his country. Gilmour handles his material well, but the book would have been strengthened by a concluding chapter that carefully evaluated the many aspects of Fraga's career. In addition, the reader learns virtually nothing about Fraga's personal life and the light it might shed on his political behavior. The book is well written and easily understood. Recommended for general readers, undergraduates, graduate students, and faculty. -- *J. M. Scolnick Jr., University of Virginia's College at Wise* **Review in 2000 Mar CHOICE**

The Imaginary in the Writing of Latin American Author Amanda Labarca Hubertson (1886-1975): Supplements to A Feminist Critique

by Sandra M. Boschetto-Sandoval

0-7734-6395-X   240pp.   2004

This postmodern feminist study seeks to rescue from ob-
scurity the literary works of the Chilean educator and
women's advocate. It is partially successful. Boschetto-
Sandoval (Michigan Technological Univ.) describes Labarca as an ambivalent feminist who both reflected and
rejected Chile's traditional, patriarchal culture. She shared
the class and race biases of her time, favoring both the
"whitening" ideal and limits on suffrage. Yet Labarca de-
sired the "feminization" of culture through a combination
of "scientific valor and maternal tenderness" that would
value women's contributions to both the public and private
spheres. Labarca was influenced by the ideas of William
James and John Dewey, whose progressive education she
sought to implant both to benefit women and to check the
influence of the church and the oligarchy. Boschetto-
Sandoval claims that the postmodern notion of the socially
constructed subject is present in Labarca's "evolutionary,"
or developmental, feminism. However, it is important not
to claim too much, for Labarca was very much a transitional figure, and one must exercise caution when viewing
her through a contemporary lens. For the most part,
Boschetto-Sandoval is cautious, drawing attention to the
hesitancies and contradictions in the writings of this educational reformer, who conforms neither to her own time
nor to the present. **Summing Up:** Recommended. Graduate and research collections. -- *D. L. Heyck, Loyola University Chicago*
Review in 2005 Jan CHOICE

The Self in the Narratives of José Donoso (Chile 1924-1996)

by Mary Lusky Friedman

0-7734-6419-0   150pp.   2004

Donoso's exploration of identity and the nature of the self is a constant theme throughout his writings. In this well-documented study, Friedman (Wake Forest Univ.) uncovers a variety of ways this signature feature manifests itself. In her lucid analysis of Donoso's fictionalized memoirs, novels, and short stories, the author demonstrates how Melanie Klein's work in psychoanalysis--especially her object-relations theories--profoundly influenced the Chilean writer and provided the conceptual framework for his psychological fiction. Donoso employs the technique of splitting and doubling of characters in order to illustrate one of his favorite motifs, the transformation of the self. In his view, the self is constructed and determined by two principal factors--the social and the psychological. He often conveys these markers by means of ambiguities of societal status, ambivalence in parent-child relations, and instances of the grotesque, all of which are on display in his best-known novel, *The Obscene Bird of Night*. Including excellent bibliographies, this important scholarly study will be of particular interest to those specializing in modern Latin American literature. **Summing Up:** Highly recommended. Graduate students, researchers, faculty. -- *M. S. Arrington Jr., University of Mississippi* **Review in 2005 Jan CHOICE**

THE NOVELS OF AGUSTÍN YÁÑEZ: A CRITICAL PORTRAIT OF MEXICO IN THE 20TH CENTURY

by Christopher Harris

0-7734-7547-8   168pp.   2000

Yáñez is best remembered as a technical innovator and novelist of the Mexican Revolution (1910-20). Harris (Univ. of Liverpool, UK) claims that Yáñez was a social critic as well--an unusual assertion considering that Yáñez held high government office and toed the PRI line for many decades. Harris's argument rests principally on Yáñez's three urban novels that denounce *caciquismo* (control by "strongmen"), corruption, and government restrictions on artistic freedom while vigorously promoting economic development as the way for Mexico to defeat bossism and modernize. He portrays Yáñez as an intellectual whose credibility, generally speaking, remained uncompromised by his loyalty to Mexico's autocratic government. Though he acknowledges that Yáñez's silence after the massacre of Tlaltelolco in 1968, in which hundreds of student protestors and others were killed by government troops, constitutes a flagrant exception to his thesis, the author maintains that, overall, Yáñez managed to walk the fine line between critical conscience and party spokesman. Although Harris's argument is only partially convincing, his book is useful for its presentation of the ethical and artistic dilemmas confronting Mexico's intellectuals, who are often caught between self-interest and more noble impulses. Especially useful for undergraduates. -- D. L. Heyck, *Loyola University Chicago*
Review in 2001 Apr CHOICE

THE LITERARY REPRESENTATION OF PERU

by James Higgins

0-7734-7277-0   336pp.   2002

Spanning more than 400 years, this study focuses on literary representation of Peruvian society as it responded to modernity. In spite of the linear approach of the chapters, the book is organized by topic; for example, in the chapter titled "The World Upside Down," Higgins (Univ. of Liverpool, UK) begins with a 16th-century Quechua poem and ends with a novel written in the 1990s. Something similar happens with other chapters. The topics Higgins addresses will be familiar to any expert on Peru. The book might have been improved by some theoretical analysis from the social sciences--e.g., as one finds in Constantin von Barloewen's *History and Modernity in Latin America: Technology and Culture in the Andes Region* (Eng. tr., 1995). Instead, Higgins treats the reader to a rich selection of quotes from a variety of poets and narrators, and even oral tradition, always directing attention to a conflictive process of change, with elites and the marginalized poor in a never-ending struggle for power and redemption. He frames this abundant material (some of it very recent), with its power to describe "social reality," within a less-than-original context. No English translations are provided for the quoted Spanish. For large collections supporting study at the advanced undergraduate level. -- *O. B. González, Loyola University of Chicago*
Review in 2002 Sept Review

A Royalist Volunteer / Un Voluntario Realista

by Benito Pérez Galdós
Translated by Lila Wells Guzmán

0-7734-9360-3   488pp.   1993

This is one of Benito Pérez Galdós's 48 historical novels treating of Spanish history during, approximately, the first three quarters of the 19th century. The present novel is the eighth volume of the second series of the famous Episodios nacionales, the source of many Spaniards' most intimate historical knowledge of the period in question. This particular volume, like the rest of the series of which it is a part, portrays "the mutinous epic" of internal strife and civil anarchy which followed the truly epic struggle to free Spain from Napoleonic domination, the subject of the first series. This volume is well translated, and is the second episodio rendered into English by Guzmán. Her endnotes and selected bibliography, as well as the introduction by the eminent Galdosian specialist Brian J. Dendle will be of use to those who need background on the historical and literary dimensions of the novel. Since the volume contains the Spanish text on left-hand pages and the English translations on facing right-hand ones, it may be used in intermediate classes of language. General readers of history and those in classes of general and world literature will also find this book of value. -- *S. Miller, Texas A&M University*
Review in 1994 Jan CHOICE

A Biography of Distinguished Scientist Gilbert Newton Lewis

by Edward S. Lewis

0-7734-8284-9   152pp.   1998

This slim but expensive volume offers a useful, brief synopsis of the career of one of the most distinguished American chemists by his son. It includes too few reminiscences of Lewis the man but does include some 20 photographs of Lewis and his family plus seven pages of appreciations by well-known scientists. Lewis pioneered in the electronic theory of valency and contributed significantly to chemical thermodynamics, especially in the studies of free energies. He is especially remembered for his very generalized definition of acids and basis; the term "Lewis acid" is now in common use in the chemical world. Full bibliography of Lewis's publications. General readers; undergraduates through faculty. -- *H. Goldwhite, California State University, Los Angeles*
Review in 1999 Mar CHOICE

AN ANNOTATED CATALOGUE OF THE ILLUSTRATIONS OF HUMAN AND ANIMAL EXPRESSION FROM THE COLLECTION OF CHARLES DARWIN: AN EARLY CASE OF THE USE OF PHOTOGRAPHY IN SCIENTIFIC RESEARCH

by Phillip Prodger

0-7734-8467-1   144pp.   1997

This annotated catalog of nearly 200 photographs--
preserved in the Darwin Papers of the Cambridge University Library--includes those used by Charles Darwin in
illustrating the similarity of facial expression between hu-
mans and other animals in his last great work of evolution,
The Expression of the Emotions in Man and Animals
(1872). The brief introduction explains that, as advances
were made in the technology of photography, it became
apparent that the best illustrations drawn by draftsmen
could not match the accuracy and detail in photographs. It
adds that Darwin was an inveterate collector who made
good use of these materials. The main part of the catalog
supplies a description of each photograph, the type of
print and negative, how it was used, its location in the
Darwin Papers, marginal notes made by Darwin, and other
information. In addition, the 30 photographs Darwin included in the first edition of *The Expression* are listed in a
separate section. This is a helpful guide for Darwin scholars; however, with the exception of the cover and the fron-
tispiece, there are no reproductions of the photographs that
assisted Darwin in constructing such a powerful argument.
Graduate students; faculty and researchers; professionals.
-- *J. S. Schwartz, CUNY College of Staten Island*
Review in 1998 July CHOICE

JAMES JOYCE AND MODERNISM: BEYOND DUBLIN

by Morton P. Levitt

0-7734-7869-8   296pp.   2000

Levitt has been a distinguished critic of James Joyce and modernism for more than three decades. This volume collects 13 essays that he has published or presented in various places over the years and affords him the privilege of commenting on his own work in retrospect. He is quick to point out that he is a humanist, not a contemporary theorist, and he defends his position as valid in the face of recent fads and trends that have taken readers' attention away from literature itself. Though Joyce is his main concern, Levitt is also a comparatist, and his subjects range from Carlos Fuentes to Nikos Kazantzakis to Paul Cezanne. The broad nature of Levitt's interests allows him to consider poetry, painting, music, and the rebirth of experimentalism in the South American novel, all in a modernist context. In general, these essays hold up well. They are informative, and often provocative, and the book stands as a solid demonstration of a scholarly career that has made a significant contribution to Joyce studies and to the field of literature. For large collections supporting the study of literature at the upper-division undergraduate level and above. -- *M. H. Begnal, Pennsylvania State University, University Park Campus*
Review in 2000 Sept CHOICE

GENDER, IDENTITY AND THE IRISH PRESS, 1922-1937: EMBODYING THE NATION

by Louise Ryan

0-7734-7298-3 320pp. 2002

Ryan (sociology, Univ. of Central Lancashire) tells a compelling story of female images in the Irish press during the formative years of the Irish Republic. Most newspapers worked with the Free State government and Catholic Church to shape a particularly moralistic brand of Irish nationalism. Essential to that nationalism were symbolic women. The revival of the Tailteann Games in honor of the ancient Celtic heroine, depictions of the "mother of many children" with spinning wheel and cozy cottage, and exemplifications of Margaret Pearse as Mother Ireland illustrate that "nationalism and nation-building are gendered projects." Female behavior that diverged from these images received only negative coverage. Thus, the Irish flapper had fallen under foreign influence (with the exception of 1920s pilots Lady Heath, Amy Johnson, and Jean Batten); the female industrial worker took men's jobs; the "emigrant girl" sacrificed the future of the Irish race; republican women "represented threats to public order and national stability"; and young women who abandoned their babies (infanticide was widespread then in Ireland) flew in the face of all moral standards of this proud nation. A must-read for all interested in Irish history and Irish women's studies. All levels. -- *C. M. McGovern, Frostburg State University*
Review in 2002 Oct CHOICE

IS JIHAD A JUST WAR?:
WAR, PEACE, AND HUMAN RIGHTS UNDER ISLAMIC AND PUBLIC INTERNATIONAL LAW

by Hilmi M. Zawati

0-7734-7304-1   244pp.   2002

This work is not as overly ambitious as the title suggests; in fact, it is brief (112 pages), limited in objective, and impressively succinct. Zawati offers a general comparison of the form of armed struggle called *jihad* with international law. His primary point is that *jihad* is not the aggressive religious war it is often purported to be; rather, it is a defensive war that meets the just-war criteria established in the United Nations Charter and other international laws of war. Zawati's argument is persuasive as a legal defense of *jihad*, but it is not intended to be a scholarly analysis, in that alternative interpretations are not considered. The most helpful aspects of Zawati's study are the correlations he draws between Islamic international law and the actual text of the Koran, the Treaty of Medina, and other primary Islamic sources. A number of these translated documents (as well as an easily understood glossary) are provided in the appendixes. These features make the book attractive to and appropriate for a wide spectrum of university-level readers, especially since it can stand alone or nicely accompany other writings on *jihad*. Recommended at all readership levels. -- *A. C. Wyman, Wilmington College*
Review in 2002 Mar CHOICE

A CRITICAL BIBLIOGRAPHY OF WRITINGS ON JUDAISM: PART 1 & 2

by David B. Griffiths

0-88946-254-2   350pp.   1989

This two-volume work covers books, articles, and even encyclopedia entries on all aspects of Jews and Judaism from ancient to modern times. It is divided into five major sections, each broken down into six to eight chapters and further subdivided into smaller units, prefaced by brief but critical and very helpful introductions. Volume 1 covers resources, (including archival sources, reference tools, etc.), the ancient Near East, the medieval period, and thought and culture (including philosophy, Kabbalah, and Hasidism). The larger Volume 2 includes the modern period with chapters on such topics as the Holocaust (and anti-Semitism), Zionism, and modernity and modern thought. The latter contains the most novel and interesting unit on "social critics and criticism." Most book entries are annotated. Although annotations are mostly descriptive, rather than critical, they are very helpful, frequently citing reviews or a work's origin as a dissertation. Frequent cross-references help avoid repetition. Very few typos or blatant errors; but the Fugu Plan is a fictionalized, popular work and no authority on the Japanese policy re the Jews. A brief comparison of the coverage of one theme, Zionism, in this work and in another excellent, related bibliography, Abraham J. and Hershel Edelheit's The Jewish World in Modern Times (CH, Jan '89), reveals that Griffiths provides about five times as many citations as the Edelheits. The one inexcusable flaw in this work of more than 800 pages is the lack of an index, or even a very detailed table of contents. The smaller Edelheit volume, on the other hand, boasts 70 pages of author, title, and subject indexes. Griffiths's publishers should issue an index volume, for this is a major reference tool, highly recommended to all libraries. -- *D. Kranzler, Queensborough Community College, CUNY*
Review in 1989 July CHOICE

THE TERRITORIAL RIGHTS OF NATIONS AND PEOPLES: ESSAYS FROM THE BASIC ISSUES FORUM

Edited by John R. Jacobson

0-88946-588-6   352pp.   1989

The reemergence of the nationalist spirit in the world today highlights the importance of this collection, which focuses on the "territorial rights of nations and peoples." The essays were selected from a competition sponsored by the Basic Issues Forum of Washington and Jefferson College. The book is divided into four logical sections: Part 1 deals with the question of territorial claims and international law. The notion of a "people" preceded the concept of the "state," creating problems in law and politics. These ideas lead into Part 2, which deals with people and artificially created political boundaries. The authors focus on the Irish, the Palestinians in the West Bank and Gaza, Scotland, Catalonia, and the Chinese nation. Part 3 deals with the abstract and normative dimensions of justice, morality, and the actual territory in question. Part 4, the highly abstract concluding section, discusses the question of how people can continue to live with one another in the world in the future. This is a book best appreciated for its sensitivity to the increasing complexity of a multicultural world. Best suited for upper-division undergraduates and graduate students interested in ethics and international politics. -- *S. R. Silverburg, Catawba College*
Review in 1990 July CHOICE

THE SONG OF ROLAND—
ON ABSOLUTES AND RELATIVE VALUES

by Marianne J. Ailes

0-7734-7229-0   196pp.   2002

Using close textual exegesis, Ailes (Wadham College, Oxford) focuses on the ethical and religious values expressed in *La Chanson de Roland*. Though it lacks the scope of standard works by scholars such as Joseph Bédier (Bedier) , Pierre Le Gentil, and Joseph Duggan, this study is nonetheless an effective contribution to understanding the poem because it concentrates on the characters of Roland, Ganelon, and Charlemagne seen in the context of their familial, feudal, and religious relationships. Ailes sets the stage by presenting the ethical framework of the poem and its absolutes of right and wrong, where loyalty to feudal lord and God are not negotiable. She then examines the individual characters who accept these absolutes but who are themselves nuanced by their human frailties and conflicting goals. The study includes a fascinating discussion of the concept of human and divine justice as shown by the trial of Ganelon and Charlemagne's victory over the Saracens. A close analysis of the terms *amur* and *amistiez* helps elucidate the complex social and political relationships in the poem. Careful references to other interpretations, a detailed bibliography, and a readable style make this book a very useful tool for lower- and upper-division undergraduates. -- *L. W. Yoder, Davidson College*
Review in 2002 Oct CHOICE

IMAGES OF HUMANIST IDEALS IN ITALIAN RENAISSANCE ART

by Charles H. Carman

0-7734-7804-3   208pp.   2000

Unpretentious and at times charmingly quixotic, this selective treatment of highlights from an old-fashioned view
of the Renaissance hits the high points: Masaccio, Leo-
nardo, Michelangelo. Carman has comprehensible and
interesting things to say, and covers the traditional bibliography respectably. On the other hand, so traditional is
the view of the Renaissance presented here, without even
a hint of defensiveness, that it seems like a manuscript
taken out of mothballs for the new millennium, to remind
us of what Renaissance studies were like in the days of
Kristeller and Wittkower. Many things can be learned
from these loosely tied essays, but a bold treatment of the
topic indicated by the title it is not. The black-and-white
photographs are serviceable. Recommended for lower-
division undergraduates. -- *P. Emison, University of New
Hampshire*
Review in 2002 Dec CHOICE

UNDERSTANDING CHAUCER'S INTELLECTUAL AND INTERPRETATIVE WORLD: NOMINALIST FICTION

by Edward E. Foster

0-7734-7972-4   252pp.   1999

Foster's solid and gracefully written explication of Chaucer's major works, the dream visions, *The Canterbury Tales*, and *Troilus and Criseyde*, sets these works within the context of 14th-century nominalism--particularly that of William of Okham, who separates the spheres of faith and abstract speculation from that of individual experience. Russell Peck made the connection between nominalism and Chaucer's fictions. Foster (Whitman College) extends this connection, arguing that totalizing interpretations cannot be set on Chaucer's inconclusive fictions. Rather, Chaucer aims, through the use of narrative techniques that self-consciously draw attention to the processes of fiction, to direct the reader's attention to the act of interpretation itself and to the exploration of the dilemmas of human experience to which the absolutes of faith do not always provide satisfying answers. The book has a slightly dated quality, relying heavily on the dramatic theory connecting teller to tale and ignoring some recent criticism such as feminist readings of the *Wife of Bath* and of *Criseyde*. Nevertheless, Foster makes a valuable contribution to the understanding of the indeterminacy of knowing in Chaucer's texts. -- *J. Cowgill, Winona State University*
Review in 2000 Apr CHOICE

Chaucer's Tragic Muse: The Paganization of Christian Tragedy

by Christine Herold

0-7734-6855-2   336pp.   2002

Herold (College of Saint Rose) dismantles the premise that Chaucer adheres to a single, simplistic paradigm for tragedy and shows how Chaucer adopts and adapts both Christian and pagan traditions. Unique to Herold's discussion of Chaucerian tragedy is her demonstration that Chaucer is indebted to the plays of Seneca and her insistence that Chaucer's understanding of classical sources is sophisticated rather than naive. Showing how Senecan tragedy prefigures Christian medieval concepts of tragedy, Herold begins her argument illustrating how the gladiators of Senecan drama experience, in their glorious deaths, something analogous to Christian transcendence of suffering. Much of the text traces Senecan influence on medieval literature and theology, and the final chapters briefly discuss Chaucer's engagement with the Senecan tradition and lay the groundwork for further studies on the topic. Copious notes, index, and bibliography. **Summing Up:** Recommended. Upper-division undergraduates, graduate students, and specialists with interests in classical, medieval, or renaissance tragedy. -- *C. P. Jamison, Armstrong Atlantic State University*
Review in 2003 July CHOICE

BODY, HEART, AND TEXT IN THE *PEARL*-POET

by Kevin Marti

0-7734-9764-1   220pp.   1991

Marti claims "the medieval man's body constituted his single most important and aesthetic framework." The prime analogate (to use the terminology of Scholastic Philosophy) is the Incarnate Body of Christ. The understanding of corporeal spatiality is organized around the "microcosm/macrocosm matrix." A book represents a body; the Bible is the prime analogate. The design of the Medieval cathedral represents a body. The center is the high altar where the body of Christ is present in the Eucharist. The Eucharist is also a microcosm: Christ is the head of the Mystical Body representing all Christians; the macrocosmic extension is that the Incarnation is the center of all history. Parts of the Cathedral like the façade can represent the Church Triumphant and Suffering as well as heaven, earth and hell. This approach is applied to the *Pearl, Sir Gawain and the Green Knight*, and *Patience*, the works of an anonymous 14th-century writer. The unity and rich diversity of each work is revealed through spatial organization based on the body. Nevertheless, the author's views are often anachronistic - e.g., the use of Emile Mersch, a Catholic theologian, to support "the body's epistemological centrality." *Gnosis* is no substitute for *pistis*, but turns the Mystical Body theology into a mere figure of speech. Levels: graduate and upper-division undergraduate. -- *J. F. O'Malley, Slippery Rock University of Pennsylvania*
Review in 1992 Apr CHOICE

LITERATURE OF SATIRE IN THE TWELFTH CENTURY: A NEGLECTED MEDIAEVAL GENRE

by Ronald E. Pepin

0-88946-316-6   150pp.   1989

In this mature study of Latin satire, Pepin moves from his earlier interest in John of Salisbury's Entheticus to subtle analyses of a humorous and influential but neglected genre of the richly productive period Charles Haskins identified in The Renaissance of the Twelfth Century (1927). The first chapter surveys generic influences of classical satire, cross-genre adaptations from nonsatirical literature, and parodic uses of liturgy and Scriptures. Four subsequent chapters focus on broader satirical themes, which encompass whole populations: kings, courtiers, bishops, as well as women. Liberal quotes and translations from Bernard of Cluny's De contemptu mundi, the poems of Hugh of Orleans, and Walter of Chatillon, and Nigel of Salisbury's Speculum stultorum are set in their cultural context. The brief bibliography cites only general studies of satire; the infinitesimal margins defy annotation. However, endnotes for each chapter are thorough, and readers may enjoy the large typeface and interlinear white space. Essential for graduate school and scholarly libraries. -- *F. K. Barasch, Bernard M. Baruch College, CUNY*
Review in 1989 Dec CHOICE

MODERN REFLECTIONS OF CLASSICAL TRADITIONS IN PERSIAN FICTION

by Mohammad Mehdi Khorrami

0-7734-6935-4   184pp.   2002

Important in postmodern literary criticism is the rejection of totalizing or universalizing narratives in the criticism of literary works. Using the ideas of "literariness" as developed by Roman Jacobson and the Russian formalists, and of "dialogism" and "polyphony" from Mikhail Bakhtin's theory of the novel, Khorrami seeks the tools and concepts for the criticism of modern (i.e., 20-21st-century) Persian fiction within the Persian literary tradition itself. Thus, he rejects the work of Western and Westernized critics and many attributions of Western influence as "neo-Orientalist discourse," which he views as generally reductionist. Avoiding the formalists' notion of literary criticism as a scientific discipline through the use of universal categories, the author develops his flexible theory in a cogent manner. He devotes the first part of the book to working out the theory and the remainder to applying his theory to a prominent novel and some short stories. He chooses his examples carefully, and his theory is accommodating enough to illuminate various fictional structures. This is a thoughtful book and an interesting contribution to postmodernist criticism of Persian fiction. **Summing Up:** Recommended. Persian and comparative literature collections serving upper-division undergraduates through faculty. --
W. L. Hanaway, emeritus, University of Pennsylvania
Review in 2003 Oct CHOICE

A CRITICAL STUDY OF THE WORKS OF NAWAL EL SAADAWI, EGYPTIAN WRITER AND ACTIVIST

by Diana Royer

0-7734-7538-9   202pp.   2001

Royer (Miami Univ.) provides one of the first book-length feminist analyses of the novels of Nawal Sa`dawi, a controversial and brilliant feminist writer and activist. She offers a sincere, at times confusing, effort to integrate cultural context and literary analysis of four of Sa`dawi's novels: *Two Women in One* (Eng. tr., 1985), *Worn at Point Zero* (Eng., 1983), *The Circling Song* (Eng., CH, Jan'90), and *God Dies by the Nile* (Eng., 1985). The final chapter draws connections between Virginia Woolf and Sa`dawi and is less than convincing. Each chapter begins by connecting myth to politics and history, then goes on to discuses their relationship to the novel discussed. Although Royer correctly looks at the underlying structure of gender relations in Egypt, it is difficult to analyze the political climate in this context from an outside perspective, in part because events move so quickly. Each chapter stands alone as an essay on a specific text, but the book lacks continuity as a whole. Useful in all large academic collections supporting world literature and women's studies classes, the book joins Fedwa Malti-Douglas's *Men, Women, and Gods* (1995), which Royer does reference, one of the only other analyses of Sa`dawi's fiction from a feminist perspective. -- *R. M. Bredin, California State University--Fullerton*
Review in 2002 Jan CHOICE

THE POLITICS AND AESTHETICS OF KATEB YACINE: FROM FRANCOPHONE LITERATURE TO POPULAR THEATRE IN ALGERIA AND OUTSIDE

by Kamal Salhi

0-7734-7871-X   448pp.   1999

Salhi does an excellent job of tracing the evolution of Ya-cine's political and aesthetic ideas, from *Nedjma* (Paris, ,1956) through the years of his permanent return to Alge-ria in 1971 until his death in 1989. From his earliest po-ems to his last performance pieces, Yacine used the same characters, situations, and incidents in his writing. The character Nedjma represents not only an obsession with an alluring but distant woman, but also an identification with Algeria, the colonized mother country attempting to re-evaluate her past and define her true identity. Yacine's plays have a characteristic rhythm that alternates between poetic and comic styles. Limited in his earlier years to the use of French to express himself in writing, Yacine played an ambiguous role in the Arabic literary renaissance (*nahdah*). In fact, Algerian theater may have been born in 1926, when Allalou wrote *Djeha* in colloquial Algerian Arabic. Yacine chose to present his plays in Algerian Ara-bic and Berber, and he made use of the *halqah*: the stage is set up as an open circle, which draws the audience into the performance. Excellent bibliography for insights into the Algerian theater. Upper-division undergraduates through professionals. -- *S. R. Schulman, Central Con-necticut State University*
Review in 2000 May CHOICE

POLITICS, POETICS AND THE ALGERIAN NOVEL

by Zahia Smail Salhi

0-7734-7957-0   304pp.   1999

Whereas most researchers believe that the first Francophone Algerian novel appeared in 1950 with the publication of Mouloud Feraoun's *Le Fils du pauvre*, Salhi (Univ.
of Leeds, UK) posits that the first actually appeared in
1908, with the publication in Paris of Seddick Ben El
Outa's *Fils de grande tente*. And whereas those who reject
the early Francophone Algerian novels argue that they
were written by a group of assimilated Algerians who be-
trayed their people's true interests and described Algerian
society as if with colonial eyes, Salhi is of the opinion that
the early novels are not only legitimate ancestors of the
novels published in the 1950s but also an important phase
in the development of the Francophone Algerian novel.
Thus, she refers to the years 1908-47 as the period of imi-
tation and assimilation, and to 1947-50 as a transitional
period. Salhi has placed such writers as Feraoun, Mohammed Dib, Mouloud Mammeri, and Kateb Yacine in the
periods of revelation, realism, alienation, and revolution.
She devotes a chapter to women in the Algerian novel of
the 1950s. Her conclusion and epilogue articulate postin-
dependence concerns. The French texts include typographical errors. Salhi includes excellent bibliographies of
primary and secondary sources and of the Francophone
Algerian novel in general. Upper-division undergraduates
through faculty. -- *S. R. Schulman, Central Connecticut
State University*
Review in 2000 July CHOICE

GENERAL WAR AMONG GREAT POWERS IN WORLD HISTORY

by Matthew Melko

0-7734-7429-3   375pp.   2001

Melko examines many of the "general wars" throughout human history and concludes, not surprisingly, that they are often related to deeper social crises, are very destructive, and, more often than not, are part of a hegemonic cycle. For the author, a general war must include at least three great powers, exist within one of 11 "mainstream civilizations," as he defines them, and must last at least two decades. Looking at 38 cases that this complex produces and the sweep of 5,000 years (from the Sumerian conflict in the third millennium BCE to the present), the work provides considerable description of the general war phenomenon found throughout time and space. This holistic study ends up not with a model, but with "a possible alternative framework" which suggests that general wars are fought one-third of the time, are more likely to end the rule of a hegemon than start one, are mostly likely to be intercivilizational, and so on. Undergraduates may find that the final 60 pages, which are devoted to useful maps and basic descriptions of the general wars, will stimulate further research. -- *C. Potholm II, Bowdoin College*
Review in 2002 Apr CHOICE

THE IMPACT OF BLACK NATIONALIST IDEOLOGY ON AMERICAN JAZZ MUSIC OF THE 1960S AND 1970S

by John D. Baskerville

0-7734-6646-0   188pp.   2003

Jazz is too often perceived only as entertainment, its social history being involved with speakeasies, bordellos, and dance clubs, with the humor of Louis Armstrong or Dizzy Gillespie. Therein rests a problem with black culture, especially as advanced by the music industry: it *is* entertaining, but if it is evaluated only on the undeniable attraction of its surface, its real essence is ignored. Certainly by the time of Billie Holiday's "Strange Fruit" (1939), jazz had overtly taken on the African heritage of social commentary. Baskerville (history, Univ. of Northern Iowa) responds to that history, not so much through his personal philosophical agenda as by scholarly documentation and interpretation. The author organizes the material carefully within the context of social issues, a process that explains the ebonization of all black music idioms--especially during the politically sensitive decades examined, not just in the US. This is a study of the *meaning* of jazz, not of its musical structure. The result is a document on aesthetics that will be thought-provoking, begging consultation certainly by musicians but not limited to them, as the bibliography indicates. **Summing Up:** Highly recommended. Upper-division undergraduates through faculty and professionals. -- *D.-R. de Lerma, Lawrence University*
Review in 2004 Mar CHOICE

ANTON BRUCKNER—
A DOCUMENTARY BIOGRAPHY:
VOLUME 1: FROM ANSFELDEN TO VIENNA;
VOLUME 2: TRIAL, TRIBULATION & TRIUMPH IN VIENNA

by Crawford Howie

Vol. 1: 0-7734-7300-9   364pp.   2002
Vol. 2: 0-7734-7302-5   432pp.   2002

Since the centenary of Bruckner's death in 1996, a great deal of research has appeared on many aspects of the Austrian composer's life
and music. Howie bases his scrupulously detailed account of Bruckner's life and music on letters, documents, contemporary reviews, and
other primary sources. Volume 1 (1824-77) covers the period from
Bruckner's birth through the early Vienna years. Howie cobbles an
enormous amount of material into a flowing narrative, shedding light
on the composer's complicated early life. He dispells many myths that
have plagued Bruckner scholarship over the years, especially those
created by Bruckner's disciples and early biographers August
Göllerich and Max Auer. For example, some less-than-glowing first-
hand accounts of recitals bring into question Bruckner's reputation as,
perhaps, the greatest organist of his day. Howie details the music from
the St. Florian and Linz days, as well as the early Vienna years, and
he provides particularly important insights into the composer's personality as articulated in letters to and from his many friends and ac-
quaintances. The volume ends with Bruckner on the verge of musical
greatness.

Volume 2 comprises the final two chapters of the biography. The volume opens in 1878, when Bruckner had become an acknowledged
master throughout Europe but had also been demonized by conservative critics. Throughout his later life, Bruckner expressed self-doubt
and was always concerned about the performance and reception of his
music. He was constantly compared to Brahms, and pejoratively tied
to the avant-garde school of Richard Wagner. Howie brings out
Bruckners insecurity and loneliness through careful examination of
letters and documents from the composer's closest confidants. Although the writing is excellent, the study lacks musical examples and
illustrative material, and the double-spaced, typed format makes for
tedious reading. Nonetheless, this substantial piece of scholarship is a
must for collections serving upper-division undergraduates and above.
-- *B. Doherty, Southwest Missouri State University*
Review in 2002 Sept CHOICE

An Interdisciplinary Study of The Ox and The Slave (Bumba-Meu-Boi): A Satirical Music Drama in Brazil

by Kazadi wa Mukuna

0-7734-6690-8   274pp.   2003

Written in a clear style free of jargon, this book introduces and analyzes from several different angles a folk drama common in Maranhão, in northwest Brazil. The presentation of this drama provides an opportunity to release aggressions through the hilarious display of social sanctions and to simultaneously express devotion to St. John, St. Peter, and St. Mark. Kazadi wa Mukuna (Kent State Univ.) first presents an argument for the origin of the drama by the slave population (contrary to many other writings), then describes and analyzes in detail the event itself, its role in the past and in current society, and its adaptation to changing musical tastes. Extensive song texts and translations, 15 photos (7 in color), 15 songs in musical notation, and a glossary complement this thorough study that gives a deeper understanding of this genre than earlier scholarship affords. **Summing Up:** Recommended. Upper-division undergraduates through faculty. -- *R. Knight, Oberlin College*
Review in 2004 Mar CHOICE

A CRITIQUE OF MUSICOLOGY: CLARIFYING THE SCOPE, LIMITS, AND PURPOSES OF MUSICOLOGY

by John A. Kimmey

0-88946-437-5   328pp.   1989

Kimmey attempts nothing less than a systematic survey of the problems of musical knowledge--practical, historical, and speculative--from classical antiquity through the late 19th century. But his book is rather more than a mere recapitulation of "musicology," by which he means any scholarly appraisal of music or its effects. On the contrary, this volume offers music historians a number of cogent observations on how writers from Aristotle to Guido Adler and from Philippe de Vitry to Francois Fetis viewed music, the art of composition, and the practical matters of performance. What interests Kimmey most, it seems, are the philosophical preconceptions that rest behind the various musical outlooks he considers. The bulk of the text is taken up with a chronological survey of ancient, medieval, Renaissance, Enlightenment, and 19th-century views of music. But this "retrospective of musicology," as Kimmey calls it, is framed by a more general "phenomenological critique" of the discipline in a philosophical sense: its methods, general limits, and its epistemology. This book does more than summarize the scholastic heritage of musical knowledge; it frames the broader project of self-examination recently proposed by a number of modern musicologists (see, for instance, Joseph Kerman's Contemplating Music: Challenges to Musicology, CH, Sep '85). Upper-division undergraduate and graduate collections. -- *R. Freedman, Haverford College*
Review in 1989 July CHOICE

A Translation of Ryôjinhishô, A Compendium of Japanese Folk Songs (Imayô) from the Heian Period (794-1185)

Translated by Gladys E. Nakahara

0-7734-6626-6   368pp.   2003

The Ryoojinhishoo provides rare insight into the lives and culture of common people in the Heian period. Songs of prostitutes, cormorant fishermen, children, gamblers, and mothers voice timeless emotions. The other scholarly monograph in English on the Ryoojinhishoo, Yung-Hee Kim's outstanding *Songs to Make the Dust Dance* (CH, Jul'94), provides a translation of 222 of the extant songs and gives a full account of Emperor Go-Shirakawa's relationship to the collection. Nakahara includes translations of all 571 extant songs, and her introduction sets the songs in the context of a masterfully reconstructed history of the folk-song genre. The previously untranslated songs include many on Buddhist themes. These songs are a priceless record of how ordinary people in the Heian period understood Buddhism; indeed, their existence refutes the notion that popular Buddhism began in the Kamakura period. Nakahara's translations, accompanied by romanized versions of the original, are fluid and well annotated. This fine work is both scholarly and imminently accessible in style and content. When the print-run of this hard-cover edition is exhausted, some press should consider it for a paperback edition. **Summing Up:** Highly recommended. All collections supporting the study of Japanese literature and culture. -- *S. Arntzen, University of Toronto*
Review in 2004 Mar CHOICE

The Themes of the German Lied from Mozart to Strauss

by Peter Russell

0-7734-7293-2   476pp.   2002

A Germanist and a professional singer, Russell (Wellington Univ., NZ) examines thematic threads in lieder from the late 18th century to the first decades of the 20th. He focuses on poems set by Schubert, Schumann, Brahms, Wolf, and Richard Strauss, but he also examines texts of important songs by other major composers (e.g., Mozart, Beethoven, Mendelssohn, Liszt). Folksong influenced many texts, and the author compares poetic themes in lieder with those in *Des Knaben Wunderhorn* and other folksong collections. These comparisons yield fascinating results; as expected, emphasis on love and spring are common to both folksong and Romantic lieder, but relatively few lieder deal with heroic deeds and violence, which are common folk ballad topics. Some topics present in 19th-century lieder, e.g., the fascination with night and the joys of wandering, are not found in folksong at all. Although Russell does not provide musical analysis, his volume is recommended for upper-division undergraduates as a supplement to Lorraine Gorrell's outstanding introduction *The Nineteenth-Century German Lied* (CH, Feb'94) and for specialists to be used in conjunction with Susan Youens's work on Schubert and Hugo Wolf. -- *D. Ossenkop, emeritus, SUNY College at Potsdam*
Review in 2002 Oct CHOICE

A History of Christian, Jewish, Muslim, Hindu, and Buddhist Perspectives on War and Peace:
Volume 1: The Bible to 1914
Volume 2: A Century of Wars

by J. William Frost

Vol. 1: 0-7734-6561-8   520pp.   2004
Vol. 2: 0-7734-6563-4   438pp.   2004

The title of these volumes accurately describes their content. Frost (emer., Swarthmore) discusses the teachings and practices of world religions from the earliest evidence to the second Gulf War. Although volume 1 provides a useful compilation of events and doctrines prior to World War I, most of the material here will be fairly familiar to students of religion. Volume 2, a detailed account and analysis of developments since 1914, will probably be of greater value to most readers. Though both volumes are encyclopedic in scope, there is relatively more about Christianity than other traditions. Frost's central concern is the power of religion to influence war, and he mentions a few individuals and groups (such as Gandhi and the Quakers) who have made effective witnesses for nonviolence; yet despite claims of peaceful intent, religion has been, all too often, little more than a halo for national or group self-interest. Nonetheless, the interrelationship of religion and war is significant for understanding both, and Frost presents this subject in an interesting and readable fashion. Extensive bibliography and footnotes. **Summing Up:** Recommended. General readers; lower-level undergraduates through faculty/researchers. -- *H. Peebles, emeritus, Wabash College*
Review in 2004 Nov CHOICE

A POLITICAL APPROACH TO PACIFISM

by Will Morrisey

Vol. 1: 0-7734-8910-X   472pp.   1996
Vol. 2: 0-7734-8910-X   460pp.   1996

CHOICE Outstanding Academic Title

Massively erudite, this work argues against absolute pacifism and "bellicism" in favor of "prudent" just-war fighting by "'American' commercial republics" into the indefinite future. Research support from the US Institute for Peace is acknowledged. The text is contained in v.1 (451 p.) and requires reference to v.2, which consists entirely of 2,229 extensive endnotes (216 p.), more than 1,500 bibliographical sources (95 p.), and a name index (37 p.). Inspired by Plato's dialogic Republic, explicitly emulated in chapter 4, Morrisey reviews arguments from antiquity to the present. His critical interpolations throughout emphasize grounds for rejection of pacifism that will be familiar to readers of this work: human nature is prone to lethal aggression; defensive killing for survival of self, society, and freedom is justified. Morrisey's uniquely comprehensive work summarizes and carries forward the long tradition of justifications for war and violence in Western political philosophy. As Leon Harold Craig notes in his study of Plato's Republic, "there is a deep relationship between philosophy and war" (The War Lover, CH, Apr'95). Recommended for war and peace collections, advanced researchers, and admirers of scholarly erudition. -- *G. D. Paige, emeritus, University of Hawaii at Manoa*
Review in 1996 Oct CHOICE

THE PHILOSOPHY OF MATHEMATICS: THE INVISIBLE ART

by W.S. Anglin

0-7734-8706-9   260pp.   1997

Anglin presents a relatively nontechnical overview of the issues central to the philosophy of mathematics. His expressed intent is accessibility for anyone involved in either mathematics or philosophy. He largely succeeds on this point, though the usual caveat applies: the philosophy of mathematics is probably best discussed by those with some degree of formal mathematical training. The expected topics--the nature and mathematical development of the infinite; ontological schools such as realms, intuitionism, formalism, and their views of mathematical objects; and the nature of mathematical truth--are all present. Additional chapters of interest are devoted to the role that mathematics plays in history, religion, and education. Anglin does a fine job of providing the reader with the proper historical perspective in which many of the philosophical problems of mathematics arose. However, in presenting a nontechnical overview of the subject, he has not achieved much depth in the presentation of most topics. Most appropriate for use in a seminar/discussion-based course. Upper-division undergraduate and graduate students. --
D. S. Larson, Gonzaga University
Review in 1997 June CHOICE

AMERICAN WOMEN PHILOSOPHERS, 1650-1930: SIX EXEMPLARY THINKERS

Edited by Therese Boos Dykeman

0-7734-9266-6   404pp.   1993

Though the lack of female presence has been noted throughout the history of philosophy, the profession still is not making students aware of this dearth. Dykeman recognizes that many woman have performed the task of philosopher but have not been recognized for it or have been seen instead as historians, poets, idealists, or mystics. Dykeman unearths the representative works of six women from the 17th to the 20th century, displaying the power and breadth of their philosophical perspicuity by setting them within the larger context of the contemporary philosophical scene. The goal is to incorporate the women in the philosophical dialogue. Each woman's writings are accompanied by an introduction with criticisms, reviews, and pertinent comments; a chronology; a bibliography of primary and secondary sources; and a defense of the term "philospher" where appropriate. This book follows in the tradition of Nancy J. Holland's Is Women's Philosophy Possible? (CH, Sep'91), Ethel M. Kersey's Women Philosphers: A Bio-critical Source Book (CH, Feb'90), Mary Ellen Waithe's three-volume History of Women Philosophers (1987-), and such journals as Resources in Feminist Research and Hypatia. It makes a significant contribution toward raising consciousness and invites students, teachers, and researchers to reflect on the long history of gender prejudice in philosophy. Recommended for all college and university libraries. -- *J. M. Boyle, Dowling College*
Review in 1994 June CHOICE

KANT'S CRITIQUE OF TELEOLOGY IN BIOLOGICAL EXPLANATION: ANTINOMY AND TELEOLOGY

by Peter McLaughlin

0-88946-275-5   204pp.   1990

A study of Kant's contribution to an issue in the philosophy of science, viz., the possibilities and limits of mechanistic reductionism in biology. McLaughlin focuses on the antinomy of judgment in the teleology part of Kant's Critique of Judgment. The first chapter states the problems of mechanistic biology in the mid-18th century, documents Kant's familiarity with the contemporary biological debate, and introduces Kant's paradoxical notion of a "natural purpose." The second chapter examines the antinomy of pure reason from the Critique of Pure Reason. The emphasis is on Kant's account of the part-whole relation and on the idea of a noumenal causality. The concluding chapter develops a controversial interpretation of the antinomy of judgment in the Critique of Teleological Judgment. McLaughlin rejects interpretations that attribute to Kant the adoption of a holistic alternative to mechanistic reductionism. According to McLaughlin, Kant offers a solution to the insufficiency of mechanistic biological explanation that is compatible with mechanism. He further emphasizes that Kant's mechanistic reductionism is not an ontological doctrine about the nature of reality but a research program that reflects the operational procedures of the human mind. Recommended for graduate-level collections with strong holdings in German philosophy. -- *G. Zoeller, University of Iowa*
Review in 1990 Dec CHOICE

EPICUREAN ETHICS: KATASTEMATIC HEDONISM

by Peter Preuss

0-7734-9124-4   288pp.   1994

This is a valuable book, a very thorough and well-
informed study of a school of moral philosophy that is
easy to neglect because so little early material has sur-
vived, and easy to despise because it is unabashedly he-
donistic. John Stuart Mill, a 19th-century Epicurean of
sorts, complains that from ancient times those who call
pleasure the good have been contemptuously likened to
swine. Preuss does a fine job defending the founder. He
discusses the ideals of aponia, or absence of toil ("we
might try to imagine the state of the gods, a state of utter
physical ease, totally alive idleness, stressless health and
well being") and ataraxia, "unperturbedness or tranquil-
lity." His main and most original point is that the Epicurean ideal is not the sort of kinetic pleasure we all think
of; it is not like eating, drinking and sex, the pleasures of
which come and go and require a waiting period for re-
turning desire. It is, rather, katastematic, "a positive self-
evaluation" in which "life itself, the existence of the self,
is seen to be good." It is continuous and, unlike kinetic
pleasure, cannot lead to misery. One wishes that Preuss
had more clearly distinguished this from all the dreary talk
of "self-esteem" and "self-image" with which we are bom-
barded today. Still, the book is essential reading for anyone seriously interested in Epicurus. Upper-division undergraduate; graduate; faculty. -- *H. L. Shapiro, University of Missouri--St. Louis*
Review in 1995 May CHOICE

PROFESSIONAL WRESTLING, THE MYTH, THE MAT, AND AMERICAN POPULAR CULTURE

by Marc Leverette

0-7734-6625-8   248pp.   2003

Leverette (media studies, Rutgers Univ.) provides a glimpse into US popular culture through the medium of professional wrestling--primarily the World Wrestling Entertainment (WWE, formerly known as the WWF). After a brief exploration of wrestling's ancient roots, he offers his own perspective on American popular culture theory and the standard postmodern symbolic debates concerning culture, civilization, Marxism, feminism, structuralism, and semiotics (signs). He also explores the landscape and linkage concerning myth, propaganda, ritual drama, and symbolic reenactment, using transnational professional wrestling characters ranging from Stone Cold, The Rock, and the Iron Sheik to Hulk Hogan. The text culminates in an exploration of professional wrestling's "low culture" pathway from the 1930s to the present, attempting to tie popular culture themes, social symbolic interaction, and professional wrestling into a descriptive case study. **Summing Up:** Optional. Graduate students in sociology, communications, and sport studies; general readers. -- *M. L. Krotee, North Carolina State University*
Review in 2004 Feb CHOICE

AN ENCYCLOPEDIA OF JACK VANCE, 20TH-CENTURY SCIENCE FICTION WRITER

by David G. Mead

0-7734-7313-0   486pp.   2002

The purpose of this set is to "list and define all the people, places, and things invented by Jack Vance for his fiction in English." The only works not covered are the four written by Vance under the pseudonym "Ellery Queen." This set results from an experiment by Mead to see whether a database system would help in analyzing a writer's works. Entries, arranged alphabetically by the first key word, consist of three pieces: a single word or phrase used by Vance in his stories, a definition based on information from Vance's various works, and a code--an abbreviation of the story or novel title. A page number indicates where the term is first found in that particular title. Easy to use and of interest where stories and novels by Jack Vance are read and collected; highly recommended. -- *W. E. Drew Jr., SUNY Agricultural and Technical College at Morrisville*
Review in 2002 Oct CHOICE

A SOURCE BOOK FOR
STRATEGIC STUDIES IN AFRICA

by S.A. Danfulani

0-7734-7545-1   280pp.   2001

Danfulani (strategic studies, Univ. of Abuja, Nigeria; Centre for International and Strategic Studies) has produced the first compilation of English and French information sources on strategic studies in Africa. Materials cited, current through 1998, range in format from monographs to articles, dissertations, memoirs, and conference papers. The work includes a list of specialized journals and specialized institutions. It ends with a study annex, which could assist scholars. Although useful for researchers and policy makers in Africa, this book will also prove valuable to upper-division undergraduate students, graduate students, and faculty of international studies. Due to its specialized focus, this work is recommended for academic libraries with large international security and national security collections. -- *N. M. Allen, University of South Florida at Sarasota*
Review in 2001 Nov CHOICE

AN EMPIRICAL REFLECTION ON THE SMILE

Edited by Millicent H. Abel

0-7734-7002-6   296pp.   2003

That Wallace Friesen and Deborah Danner wrote the preface for this book speaks well of it. Along with Paul Ekman, Friesen is considered one of the great researchers in the field of nonverbal research. Abel (Western Carolina Univ.) offers a collection of well-conceived articles focusing on a complex nonverbal behavior--the smile--among them, "What Do Smiles Mean?" by Jo Ann Abe, Michael Beetham, and Carrol Izard (Izard stands with Ekman and Friesen as a giant in the field of nonverbal behavior). All the articles are well written and on the cutting edge of research. However, this reviewer suggests that the smile needs to be considered within the context of all other nonverbal stimuli present with that smile if one is to understand its interpersonal impact with clarity. **Summing Up:** Recommended. Lower-division undergraduates through faculty. -- *M. W. York, University of New Haven*
Review in 2003 Mar CHOICE

JUNGIAN ARCHETYPES IN 20TH CENTURY WOMEN'S FICTION: THE PERSONA, THE SHADOW, THE ANIMUS, AND THE SELF

by Lorelei Cederstrom

0-7734-7059-X   304pp.   2002

The late Cederstrom understood the irony of taking a strongly feminist view of women's fiction of the last quarter of the 20th century through the lens of a major psychological theorist ... who was male. She offers her rationale at the beginning of this thorough and deep look at fiction by women during an era when women writers were being published and recognized and were blossoming into dominance in the genre. The book's subtitle accurately outlines the Jungian archetypes Cederstrom examines. She was well read, and her discussion is intelligent. Though perhaps she does not offer any fresh insights into Jung's work, her use of Jung's archetypal theories provides insights into a large number of novels by prominent women writers. **Summing Up:** Recommended. Graduate students and faculty. *-- Q. Grigg, emeritus, Hamline University* **Review in 2003 Mar CHOICE**

JUNG'S THREE THEORIES OF RELIGIOUS EXPERIENCE

by J. Harley Chapman

0-88946-245-3   192pp.   1989

Chapman greatly clarifies Jung's understanding of religious experience by making explicit three different models or theoretical approaches Jung employed at various times in his lifelong grappling with this issue. Chapman calls these models the scientific-psychological, the phenomenological-mythological, and the metaphysical-theological. While Jung himself claimed that he was a scientist using scientific methodology, and a phenomenologist of religious experience, he repeatedly denied any role as a metaphysician or theologian. Chapman skillfully shows how Jung made, at times, metaphysical and theological statements and assumptions. His analysis of Jung's use of scientific and phenomenological methodologies are equally illuminating. This well-written work is a very important one for a fuller understanding of Jung's many writings. Its brilliance and usefulness can best be appreciated by those who have a thorough knowledge of Jung and a background in philosophy, particularly phenomenology. For graduate libraries. -- *A. McDowell, Ithaca College* ***Review in 1989 May CHOICE***

BIBLIOGRAPHY ON PSYCHOLOGICAL TESTS USED IN RESEARCH AND PRACTICE IN SPORT AND EXERCISE PSYCHOLOGY

by Arnold LeUnes

0-7734-7001-8   344pp.   2002

LeUnes's bibliography assists researchers, practitioners, and students investigating the psychology of sport and exercise by providing a reference source that both identifies and categorizes relevant assessment inventories and cites related research. The book includes 2,287 references by more than 30,000 contributors, covering 73 psychometric instruments, 65 sports, and 18 sports-related categories. The numbered citations are listed alphabetically under major types of assessment devices, including "Measures of Enduring Traits" (e.g., aggression, authoritarianism/Machiavellianism, locus of control, optimism/pessimism, self-concept/self-esteem/self-actualization, sensation seeking), "Measures of Temporary States" (anxiety/depression/mood), "Sport-Specific Measures" (aggression, anxiety, group cohesion/leadership, motivation), and "Measures of Response Tendencies" (Marlowe-Crowne Scale of Social Desirability). The 73 assessment instruments are listed in the table of contents under the appropriate trait in each section; the inclusion of an alphabetical index by test name would have been useful. The final two chapters are indexes by sport and by author. The author has been involved with research on the psychometric assessment of athletes for over 35 years and has published extensively in the field, making him a highly qualified compiler. **Summing Up**: Recommended. Upper-division undergraduates through faculty. -- *J. P. Miller, Texas A&M University*
Review in 2003 Mar CHOICE

SPIRITUAL SONNETS

by Juan Ramon Jimenez

Translated by Carl W. Cobb

0-7734-8889-8   136pp.   1996

One of Spain's great poets of the 20th century, Jimenez won the Nobel prize for literature in 1956. His reputation has suffered recently, so this translation will help to make him known to English speakers. Cobb, critic and translator of Lorca's verse, places the 55 sonnets offered here in a convenient format for English and Spanish readers: the Spanish on the left and the translation on the right. There is little scholarly apparatus--no notes or bibliography, and only a short and informal preface. Although the careful reader will miss an explanation of the translator's process, they will see that Cobb chose to retain the form of the English sonnet. The choice carries some difficulties. What is missing in English is the feeling of ordinariness that characterizes Jimenez's poetry; even in the restrictive form of the sonnet, the Spanish sounds natural and uses an everyday vocabulary. Still, Cobb's translations are thoughtful and express the poet's feelings. Recommended for all libraries. *-- R. W. Winslow, emeritus, Lawrence University* **Review in 1996 July CHOICE**

SELECTED POEMS OF ANDREE CHEDID

Translated & edited by Judy Cochran

0-7734-2908-5   224pp.   1995

The motif double-pays, or dual country, is central to this bilingual presentation of Chedid's poetry. Born in Lebanon, raised in Cairo, and a resident of France since the late 1940s, Chedid has made those multiple points of geographical reference integral to her writing. Her work includes novels, short stories, and drama, as well as poetry. However, as Cochran argues, Chedid's poems are basic to her literary creativity. Cochran has translated selections from Chedid's poetic oeuvre (1949-86) and highlights several of the themes that have been sustained throughout that literary itinerary: the dual country, to be sure, but also women's liberation and individual liberty, the travails of a war-torn Beirut, and the power of words and the integrity of language to evoke those compelling issues. The poems are elegantly translated from the French, and the volume includes a brief biographical preface and a literary and critical introduction. Recommended for all libraries, especially those with significant poetry collections. -- *B. Harlow, University of Texas at Austin*
Review in 1996 June CHOICE

The Contemplative Poetry of Edwin Arlington Robinson, Robert Frost, and Yvor Winters

by Richard Hoffpauir

0-7734-7198-7   280pp.   2002

For Hoffpauir (Univ. of Alberta, retired), contemplative
poetry is poetry that reveals a poet's mental processes,
placing emphasis on thinking over reason. Further, it has
an underlying current of ethical and moral concerns. The
author sees Robinson as conflicted between religion
(hope) and science (realism). Contemplation for Robinson
can give rise to principles for a moral and critical life.
Hoffpauir considers Frost a somewhat marginal figure in
20th-century contemplative poetry. His poetry is not as
stable and purposeful as Robinson's; he is concerned with
thinking but not so far as it results in well-shaped ideas.
Hoffpauir considers Winters the one poet to cultivate the
idea that poetry is contemplation. Winters believed that a
poet should be a kind of moral philosopher. His major
concern was with the grounds of morality itself. Throughout the book Hoffpauir examines style as a concomitant of
a poet's thinking. No comparable study exists, but useful
collateral reading may be found in Arthur Clements's *Poetry of Contemplation: John Donne, George Herbert,
Henry Vaughan, and The Modern Period* (1990). Upper-
division undergraduates and graduate students interested
in the subject will find Hoffpauir informative and at times
provocative. -- *J. J. Patton, emeritus, Atlantic-Cape Community College*
Review in 1996 June CHOICE

THE RESURGENCE OF TRADITIONAL POETIC FORM AND THE CURRENT STATUS OF POETRY'S PLACE IN AMERICAN CULTURE

by Kevin Walzer

0-7734-7554-0   192pp.   2001

Walzer is the author of *The Ghost of Tradition: Expansive Poetry and Postmodernism* (CH, Jul'99), the editor (with Kevin Bezner) of *The Wilderness of Vision: On the poetry of John Haines* (1996), and a published poet himself (*Living in Cincinnati*, 1995). Divided into two parts--the "culture of poetic forms" and the "forms of poetic culture"--the present collection of 14 wide-ranging essays continues Walzer's exploration of the resurgence of traditional verse forms and especially the rise of new formalism. Walzer discusses numerous poets--including Cummings, Millay, Stevens, James Weight, Hayden Carruth, Rita Dove, John Haines, and even Judson Jerome (poetry columnist for *Writer's Digest*). The conceptual model he uses to orient his discussion derives from the conservative work of David Ray Griffin (*God and Religion in the Postmodern World*, CH, Jun'89), especially his concept of "constructive postmodernism" (an attempt to revalorize the relationship between language and foundationalism), and the work of Frederick Turner, in particular his optimistic version of constructive postmodernism, "natural classicism." Recommended for libraries intent on comprehensive collections of criticism of late 20th-century American poetry and its internal debates. -- *D. Garrison, University of Tennessee at Chattanooga*
Review in 2001 Nov CHOICE

ROGER WILLIAMS, GOD'S APOSTLE OF ADVOCACY: BIOGRAPHY AND RHETORIC

by Raymond L. Camp

0-88946-679-3 240pp. 1989

Camp, who teaches speech communications, focuses on Roger Williams as a rational and persuasive rhetorician. He examines Williams's education in the English forensic and scholastic traditions, argues that Williams was influenced by the English jurist Edward Coke in developing his advocacy skills, and assesses the form and style of Williams's spoken and written rhetoric. Chapters 1-3 explore Williams's boyhood and education and provide the background for later chapters. These contain the heart of Camp's analysis of Williams's correspondence as written discourse, and of his 1635 sedition trial in Boston and his 1672 debates with the Quakers in Rhode Island as oral discourse. Camp explains how Williams developed and used his persuasive talents, something Perry Miller's Roger Williams (1953) and John Garrett's Roger Williams (1970) fail to address. Camp revises William Hunt's assessment of Williams in The Puritan Movement (CH, Oct '83), which pictures Williams as an irrational advocate. Footnotes, a full index, note on sources, but no bibliography. Upper-division undergraduates and above. -- *M. L. Dolan, Northern Michigan University*
Review in 1989 Nov CHOICE

THE CHRISTADELPHIANS IN NORTH AMERICA

by Charles H. Lippy

0-88946-647-5   320pp.   1989

Lippy (Clemson University), coeditor of the Encyclopedia
of the American Religious Experience CH, May '88), here
offers the first book-length study of American Christadel-
phianism. Restorationist, pacifist, nonhierarchical, and
awaiting the imminent second coming of Christ, the
roughly 6,000 North American Christadelphians (Brethren
of Christ) eschew contact with their secular neighbors and
avoid association with other Christian groups. Lippy reads
their history as a tale of passionate commitment to purity
at all costs, and he suggests that their continued existence
poses a challenge to the usual sociological analyses of sec-
tarian behavior. Though he chooses not to discuss the economic, social, and cultural lives of actual Christadelphians, Lippy's account is patient and sympathetic in describing what it means to live, as Christadelphians put it,
"in the truth." Level: graduate and upper-division undergraduate. -- *L. B. Tipson, Gettysburg College*
Review in 1990 June CHOICE

A BIBLIOGRAPHY OF SOURCES IN CHRISTIANITY AND THE ARTS

by Daven Michael Kari

0-7734-9094-9   773pp.   1995

Kari (humanities, California Baptist College) has compiled a list of 5,200 bibliographies or books containing
substantial bibliographies. Items were selected if they explore the fine arts and Christianity, with preference given
to current works. English-speaking researchers are the target audience, and only a few titles in other languages are
included. The volume is divided into broad groupings:
aesthetics, architecture, cinema, dance, drama, radio/tv,
fabric art, literature, music, photography, visual arts, and
humor. Under each category Kari first lists bibliographies,
then key works in that discipline. Cross-references are included for multidisciplinary titles, and there are author and
title indexes. Although little has been written relating
some subjects (e.g., film) to Christianity, this bibliography
of bibliographies is broader in scope than one might ex-
pect. Nonetheless, it is recommended only for libraries
that have faculty or upper-division students doing research
in this field. -- *E. Peterson, Montana State University*
Review in 1995 Sept CHOICE

A BIBLIOGRAPHY OF SALVATION ARMY LITERATURE IN ENGLISH (1865-1987)

by R. G. Moyles

0-88946-827-3   250pp.   1988

Moyles (English, University of Alberta, and Salvation
Army historian), has now compiled a bibliography of the
Salvation Army, spanning the years 1865-1987. It aims at
comprehensiveness, including primary and secondary
sources, books and articles, and even encompasses novels,
plays, and poetry about Salvation Army personnel.
Ephemera (congress programs, local brochures, sheet music) are not included. Arrangement is by nine subjects.
Three of the subject areas are further subdivided by specific topic, and all are finally arranged chronologically.
Subject sections begin with the very general (histories) to
specific (prison services, promotional literature, and so
forth). There are no annotations to the bibliographic entries, but each section has a brief overview of the topic.
An author index is supplied. Especially since there is no
other bibliography of the Salvation Army available, this
volume is recommended for reference collections with an
emphasis on religion or church history. -- *E. Peterson,
Gonzaga University*
Review in 1989 Jan CHOICE

EMERSON AND ZEN BUDDHISM

by John G. Rudy

0-7734-7461-7   294pp.   2001

Like many other titles in this Mellen series, Rudy's volume defies definition as a straightforward piece of literary
analysis. Emerson had an understanding and appreciation
of Buddhism, and Rudy considers Emerson not as a literary essayist and poet but as a spiritual guide for contemporary readers. He sees parallels between Emerson's im-
plied lessons and his preferred state of consciousness with
those of Zen Buddhism. Rudy's book is not an examination of the influence of Eastern thought on Emerson. Such
a study was written as early as 1932 by Arthur Christy
(*The Orient in American Transcendentalism*). Instead, focusing on Emerson's major essays, Rudy shows how Emerson's mind worked in similar ways to those of the Zen
masters. Both Emerson and the Zen masters did the spiritual work of "emptying" in striving to achieve what the
Buddhists call "nonattachment." Rudy works to establish a
dialog between the East and the West through Emerson
and implies a validation of the meditative dynamics of
"voidist" spirituality by finding connections between the
two. Like Richard Geldard's *The Esoteric Emerson: The
Spiritual Teaching of Ralph Waldo Emerson* (1993),
Rudy's book updates Emerson for the contemporary
seeker. Upper-division undergraduates through faculty. --
P. J. Ferlazzo, Northern Arizona University
Review in 2002 Mar CHOICE

THE MASTER AND THE DEVIL: A STUDY OF MIKHAIL BULGAKOV

by Andrzej Drawicz
Translated by Kevin Windle

0-7734-7500-1   384pp.   2001

Competently translated from the Polish, this is an interesting study of the life and work of a man who has emerged as a major Russian writer of the 20th century. Although Drawicz's account tends to be descriptive, factographic, and discursive, he makes many important points about Bulgakov's literary development. He notes that Bulgakov's fascination with the devil is of Gogolian origin--the devil symbolized "the mysterious nature of the world" and represented a natural phenomenon in an alien and hostile world--and probably turned into an obsession in the light of the revolutionary period and after, when Bulgakov nurtured a visceral disdain for communist life. Drawicz also shows how Bulgakov's works reflect various facets of his life and find ultimate synthesis in his greatest work, *The Master and Margarita*. In discussing that work, Drawicz cannot reach any "conclusive answer" concerning its "overall scheme," and he compares it to Boris Pasternak's *Doctor Zhivago* in offering "spiritual freedom to the individual." This reviewer would have found useful a discussion of the moral and ethical issues that the novel raises in the universal conflict between good and evil. Nevertheless, this is a very informative study that complements Anthony Wright's *Mikhail Bulgakov: Life and Interpretations* (CH, Jan'79). Upper-division undergraduates and above. -- *V. D. Barooshian, Wells College*
Review in 2002 Mar CHOICE

Contemporary Russian Myths: A Skeptical View of the Literary Past

by Yuri Druzhnikov

0-7734-8161-3   340pp.   1999

Druzhnikov (Univ. of California, Davis) seemingly rises to the challenge of Victor Terras ("Puskin's Prose Fiction in a Historical Context," *Puskin Today*, ed. by David Bethea, 1993) to establish how much of the reputation of Pushkin's prose relies on the enormous attention of his ingenious readers and his total stature. Druzhnikov takes as his point of departure philosophical skepticism, not literary criticism per se, pointed deliberately at the aftershock of Stalinism. He introduces doubt in the power of truth in the face of many forms of persuasion, and he echoes the skepticism of Nietzsche in *The Will to Power*: "What is needed above all is an absolute skepticism toward all inherited concepts." Druzhnikov balances this with the modern realization that concepts are not only inherited but manufactured, manipulated and, sometimes, made into weapons for the profiteers or icons for the ideologues. Also (as in Nietzsche) the idea that one true exegesis will obtain is not upheld. Druzhnikov nonetheless vigorously introduces the benefit of doubting disembodied myths and perpetuating hero-worship, using a wealth of absolutely specific details, successfully conjuring embodied personae in a material world. While rerolling the camera of history, he maintains a whimsy appropriate to the task of questioning the moot. Upper-division undergraduates and above. -- *C. Tomei, Columbia University*
Review in 1999 Dec CHOICE

A BIBLIOGRAPHY OF ALEXANDER PUSHKIN IN ENGLISH: STUDIES AND TRANSLATIONS

by Lauren G. Leighton

0-7734-8170-2   336pp.   1999

Leighton describes this bibliography as one of the English-language products of the bicentennial observance of Pushkin's death and as an updating of *Pushkin in English*, produced by the Slavonic Section of the New York Public Library (1937). The compiler claims that the work contains 250 items that have not appeared in previous bibliographies, and estimates that some 1,700 studies and 900 translations of Pushkin's works have appeared through 1997. The bibliography accordingly has two main parts, Studies and Translations. Studies, arranged alphabetically by author, is subdivided into general and specific, with sections on verse works, drama, prose, and individual works. It also contains an interesting section on translation studies. The Translations section is organized into general collections, Pushkin collections, and individual works: lyric poetry, tales, narrative verse, drama, and prose. Both sections are comprehensive; for example, Leighton lists eight translations of the famous lyric "I Loved You" and 20 of *The Bronze Horseman*. The order of tales in the subsection on translations of individual folk tales differs from the order in the table of contents. Upper-division undergraduate and graduate students. -- *R. Seitz, Eastern Illinois University*
Review in 1999 Oct CHOICE

RELIGION IN RUSSIA AFTER THE COLLAPSE OF COMMUNISM: RELIGIOUS RENAISSANCE OR SECULAR STATE

by Kimmo Kääriäinen

0-7734-8283-0   216pp.   1998

Kääriäinen (Univ. of Helsinki) first presents a succinct but useful description of the religious situation in Russia before the October Revolution, and then examines religiousness at the end of the communist regime, demonstrating a growing contradiction between the communist ideal and Soviet reality. Finally, Kääriäinen presents an intriguing exploration of religious dimensions (belief, knowledge, practice, experience, institutional and ethical effects) in postcommunist Russia. Among the primary sources used are three World Value Surveys conducted in Russia between 1991-1996. Because these sources focus on the traditional Christian (Orthodox) population, there is little in this book about Muslims or non-Orthodox Christian groups. The author adopts a methodology that treats religiousness as a composite phenomenon of multiple dimensions. These dimensions become the framework for interpreting the survey data, which are presented in narrative form and in 50 data tables. There are 250 footnotes, a nine-page bibliography, and a three-page index. Kääriäinen provides valuable information about the religiousness of people in Russia that was heretofore unavailable. Highly recommended. Lower-division undergraduates through faculty and researchers. -- *R. L. Massanari, Alma College*
Review in 1999 Apr CHOICE

RUSSIAN NATIONALISM FROM AN INTERDISCIPLINARY PERSPECTIVE: IMAGINING RUSSIA

by Daniel Rancour-Laferriere

0-7734-7671-7   364pp.   2000

Rancour-Laferriere (Univ. of California, Davis) addresses Russian national *identity*, a subject appropriate to the psychology that readers have come to associate with his works. A Freudian approach ties this study to the author's *Mind of Stalin* (1988) and *The Slave Soul of Russia* (CH, Sep'95). However, true to the strangely inverted title, extensive notes and bibliography testify to impressive scholarship ranging across many academic disciplines. Asserting that "the individual Russian *imagines* Russia," Rancour-Laferriere repeatedly reminds us that there is a reality from which imagination may deviate, wildly in some notable cases. The book is divided into two parts, each rich in insight and information: "The Russian Self" (who the Russians think they are); and "The Russian Other" (what they think concerning non-Russians). Readers interested in the excesses of Russian nationalism will not be disappointed, but essentially this fascinating book is optimistic. It concludes with the observation that, beneath the chaos of post-Soviet times, millions of individual Russians are shedding the "moral masochism" that, down through the ages, has constituted the weakest element of the national character. The more readers already know about Russia, the more Rancour-Laferriere will reward them; so this book is especially appropriate for advanced undergraduates, graduate students, and professors. -- *E. A. Cole, Grand Valley State University*
Review in 2001 Oct CHOICE

PROMOTING DEMOCRACY IN THE POST-SOVIET REGION

by Derek S. Reveron

0-7734-7148-0   244pp.   2002

Reveron studies the US State Department's program called Community Connections. The breakup of the USSR created an unprecedented window of opportunity for the US to promote democracy across the post-Soviet republics. Community Connections projects have been a milestone on the road to achieve this objective. Reveron discusses the legislative basis for the Washington democratization policy as well as the connection between the American assistance and the US Congress's positive attitude toward a people-to-people assistance project similar to Community Connections. The author also analyzes a people-to-people democratization program, including how it was put to work. Evidently, this approach proved to be successful. Otherwise, one cannot explain the fact that it had grown dramatically from $1 million annual program for Russia in 1993 to a $14 million program for eight former Soviet republics in 2001. Reveron points out that in just seven years the funding increased fifteen-fold. According to Reveron, by the year 2000, almost 1,800 entrepreneurs, educators, and NGO officials visited the US. It should be also mentioned that the author used a 144-question survey of the American organizations that receive Community Connections grants to explain the program. **Summing Up:** Recommended. Researchers, faculty, and professionals. -- *Y. Polsky, West Chester University of Pennsylvania* ***Review in 2003 July CHOICE***

FIVE EARLY WORKS
by Par Lagerkvist

Translated by Roy Arthur Swanson

0-88946-019-1   200pp.   1989

Like the late Samuel Beckett, Lagerkvist was a relentless
and merciless diagnoser of the human condition. Both
mixed their depiction of absurdity with glum humor; like-
wise, both abhorred systems of any kind, though Beckett
might not have minded Lagerkvist's saying "I am a religious atheist." That waiting for someone--be it Godot or
some (seedy) redeemer--can be detected in a great many
of their works. The present volume gathers some of
Lagerkvist's early works: short stories, sketches, essays,
and a play--all of which illustrate the young author's relationship and response to expressionism. A lengthy and
very informative introduction includes, besides an analyti-
cal commentary on Lagerkvist's technique, some samples
of the writings of the very young schoolboy and a very
useful bibliography of Lagerkvist's early publications
(1905-20). Two translators' prefaces expand on the points
made in the introduction--and it ought to be added that the
translations of the texts are meticulous and fine-tuned, to
the point that they no longer read like translations. These
texts may not have the immediate existential appeal of
such later works as Barabbas (1951) or The Dwarf (1945),
but they are much more than juvenilia, for they show a
young author who is about to master his craft. A useful
purchase for academic and public libraries. -- *N. Ing-
wersen, University of Wisconsin--Madison*
Review in 1990 Apr CHOICE

Shakespeare's Philosophy of History Revealed in a Detailed Analysis of *Henry V* and Examined in Other History Plays

by Ronald A. Rebholz

0-7734-6572-3   236pp.   2003

Rebholz (emer., Stanford) argues that the apparently conflicting impressions of Henry V can be understood by
viewing him as a Machiavellian with a conscience, and that
this blend allowed Shakespeare to express nostalgia for a
chivalric past while accepting the reality of the corrupt but
inescapable present. Although Rebholz's reading is detailed
and historically grounded, it is not as original as he believes, and when he attempts to apply this reading to other
plays, he oversimplifies. For example, he mentions *King
Richard III* only briefly. Rebholz's attempt to cover the Roman plays, including *Troilus and Cressida* and *Coriolanus*,
requires very selective readings to match his chosen pat-
tern. Two final chapters, not well connected to the earlier
argument, consider the relationship between Shakespeare's
plays with, first, providence and, second, the politics of
Elizabeth and James. The book is useful for the first chapter's discussion not only of Henry V but also of the long-
running debate on whether the title character is an admira-
ble hero or a despicable criminal; here Rebholz presents a
nuanced argument reflecting and explaining the ambivalence of most readers. **Summing Up:** Optional. Undergraduate collections. -- *A. Castaldo, Widener University*
Review in 2004 May CHOICE

The Genesis of Shakespeare's Merchant of Venice

by Christopher Spencer

0-88946-930-X   150pp.   1989

In this thorough study of the components that became Shakespeare's play, Spencer discusses sources, plot elements, character types and the attitudes toward them, stage history, and criticism. He analyzes the flesh-bond and casket stories of the plot, the characters Shakespeare added beyond his sources, and the dramatist's arrangement of scenes. Much of the discussion, of course, deals with Shylock, not merely as Jew and usurer, but especially as a vivid role to be interpreted in terms of the needs of the plot. Spencer's "conclusion that Shakespeare intended a full use of the possibilities of the role" is not surprising, but it does offer a performance-oriented corrective to one-sided presentations of the character. The notes and selected bibliography offer an extensive survey of both older and recent criticism for the use of advanced students and scholars. -- *R. E. Burkhart, Eastern Kentucky University* **Review in 1989 Oct CHOICE**

A Comparative Study of Societal Influences on Indigenous Slavery in Two Types of Societies in Africa

by E.S.D Fomin

0-7734-7225-8   284pp.   2002

This short (150 pages of text with wide margins) case study uses the numerous figures, chapter notes, foreign terms, and internal structure and style of the slightly revised dissertation that it began as 20 years earlier at the University of Yaounde, Cameroons. The author examines two types of societies selected from the centralized communities of the interior western grasslands of the Cameroons and from the "stateless" communities of the coast. This socioanthropological analysis shows that the differences in the structure and conditions of slavery depended on the underlying differences in the structures of the historical communities in which slavery existed. An important component of the research used here is years of oral data gathering in the communities studied. Upper-division undergraduates and above. -- *R. T. Brown, formerly, Westfield State College*
Review in 2002 Dec CHOICE

THE EVOLUTION OF THE LIBERAL DEMOCRATIC STATE WITH A CASE STUDY OF LATINOS IN SAN ANTONIO, TEXAS

by Henry Flores

0-7734-6674-6   248pp.   2003

CHOICE Outstanding Academic Title

Flores (St. Mary's University) shows a masterful command of the literature on the theory of the state in this example of outstanding scholarship. The most significant contribution of this volume is the application of chaos theory from the natural sciences, which creates a broad theoretical framework to better understand both theories of the state and Latino and American politics. In reminding readers of the paramount role of the nexus of the private and public sectors, associated impact of ideology, and the nature of a structured liberal democratic American state, Flores demonstrates, despite the seemingly dynamic and responsive nature of the state, why Latinos may very well continue to realize potentially overwhelming obstacles and resistance to full and real political participation in useful public policy development in the US. Very useful preface, index, and impressive bibliography. **Summing Up:** Highly recommended. Undergraduate and graduate students, researchers, faculty, and policy makers. -- *A. A. Sisneros, University of Illinois at Springfield*
Review in 2004 May CHOICE

THE SOCIOLOGY OF LAW:
A BIBLIOGRAPHY OF THEORETICAL LITERATURE
(2nd Edition)

by A. Javier Treviño

0-7734-8318-7   220pp.   1998

CHOICE Outstanding Academic Title

Treviño's superb bibliography is organized around themes
that place the theoretical literature of the sociology of law
in both historical context and comparative perspective.
The table of contents reads like a wonderful course out-
line. The first heading indicates that the materials deal
with definitional problems within the concept of law and
the sociology of law; subsequent headings identify major
schools of sociolegal thought, and subheadings treat leading figures or subschools of thought. To his credit, the author has not sought to be comprehensive in his bibliographical coverage, but has used excellent judgment in
selecting a relatively small number of the best and most
enduring articles in each area. This will prevent the book
from becoming dated for some time. Anyone teaching a
theoretically inclined course in the sociology of law could
easily turn the table of contents into a syllabus, then con-
struct a set of readings for the course by selecting articles
listed under each topic. This bibliography should be of
immense value to scholars, and to students who want to
quickly locate major writings on major topics in the field.
Despite its value for bibliographical reference on a
scholar's bookshelf, works like this should be among the
earliest candidates for electronic publication. -- *M. M.
Feeley, University of California, Berkeley*
Review in 2004 May CHOICE

COVERING SEX, RACE, AND GENDER IN THE AMERICAN MILITARY SERVICES

by Gene Murray

0-7734-6548-0   182pp.   2003

Using informal content analysis, Murray (communication, Grambling State Univ.) examines how the media covers sex, race, and gender issues in the US military and investigates the perceptions of future equal opportunity advisors. After a perfunctory overview of US media roles and a somewhat indiscriminate endorsement of media social responsibility theory, Murray presents his research in three related chapters. The first focuses on the extensive media coverage of sexual harassment in the military and finds that equal opportunity advisors are concerned with the negative impact on recruitment, and that African American equal opportunity advisors are more likely to believe that racism is involved in sexual harassment. The second deals with equal opportunity and officer progression, and finds that media coverage of two Department of Defense reports was generally balanced, with a tendency to emphasize stories about minority encounters with racism. The third examines press coverage of gender-integrated training and finds most columnists writing in favor of the practice. The survey research finds that male and female equal opportunity advisors favor such training, although females were more likely to agree that double-standards were applied during training. Media scholars and researchers with an interest in equal opportunity issues will find this book useful. **Summing Up:** Recommended. Most academic collections. -- *G. B. Osborne, University of Alberta*
Review in 2004 Sept CHOICE

A CONCISE HISTORY OF POLISH THEATER FROM THE ELEVENTH TO THE TWENTIETH CENTURIES

by Kazimierz Braun

0-7734-6791-2   532pp.   2003

Braun (SUNY, Buffalo), a native of Poland, remains a vital force in the Buffalo theater community. His new book is, by his own admission, narrative in style, and the narration profits from the richness of Braun's theatrical knowledge and experiences in Eastern Europe and America. Again by his admission, Braun attempts to make the book, designed for English-speaking readers, "reader-friendly": he has translated all Polish titles and names of theaters in Poland into English, keeping intact the names of people and geographical places. He has avoided notes that would disturb the flow of the narrative, compensating with an extensive bibliography instead. The book clarifies how Polish theater has no counterpart in the Anglo-American tradition; it focuses on Polish theater itself rather than on its opera, ballet, or other theater genres. Because of its impressive size and its rare topic, it reminds one strongly of Czeslaw Milosz's *The History of Polish Literature* (1969; 2nd ed., 1983). The sections "Theatre in Poland under Foreign Rule" and "Theatre at the Time of National Catastrophes" would strongly appeal to readers interested in both theater and the impact of WW II and its historical aftermath on the arts. **Summing Up:** Recommended. Upper-division undergraduates and above; general readers. -- *J. A. Dompkowski, Canisius College*
Review in 2004 Jan CHOICE

THEATER DIRECTING: ART, ETHICS, CREATIVITY

by Kazimierz Braun

0-7734-7828-0   544pp.   2000

Braun's career has spanned decades and continents, and
this personal (and lengthy) narrative reveals his life in the
theater as director, teacher, and creative artist. Braun's
perspective on "creative directing" finds its origins in an
eastern European sensibility: it is intellectual and highly
creative, but nonetheless remarkably disciplined. Note-
worthy is Braun's loyalty to the script at hand and his
analysis of the text. Though much of this volume focuses
on the dramatic theater, its content is relevant across a
range performance genres, including opera and musicals.
Braun provides an excellent analysis of the use of space
and the environment of the play, and he blends the efforts
of the creative artist and the practical craftsman in an intriguing way. His vision for the young director is that of
guide for both actor and spectator. This book will have a
narrow audience: it is for the serious student of directing,
either in an academic setting or in the professional theater
world. An interesting guide to finding one's own artistry in
both the art and craft of directing for the stage, it will interest professionals and the occasional upper-division undergraduate and graduate student pursuing directing. -- *J.
H. Conger III, Northern Kentucky University*
Review in 2000 Nov CHOICE

THE THEATRICAL WORKS OF GIOVACCHINO FORZANO– DRAMA FOR MUSSOLINI'S ITALY

by C.E.J. Griffiths

0-7734-7726-8   328pp.   2000

Hugely popular in Italy between the world wars but today almost completely forgotten, the work of Giovacchino Forzano--dramatist, stage director, librettist, and sometime theatrical collaborator with none other than Mussolini--is restored to scholarly attention in this thorough and consistently readable account, the first monograph on Forzano to appear in English. Drawing extensively on archives, correspondence, and contemporary newspapers, and providing detailed analysis of the most significant of Forzano's works, Griffiths (Manchester Univ., UK) skillfully situates the author's voluminous output in the cultural context of Fascist Italy, identifying its major thematic preoccupations and showing that both its composition and its reception were much more complex affairs than the understandably dismissive postwar critical consensus would imply. Griffiths includes a previously unpublished drama written in 1937, *Racconti d'autunno, d'inverno e di primavera*, in an appendix. Although clearly not a major dramatist, Forzano emerges from this lucid and well-argued discussion as a figure of considerable interest in 20th-century Italian cultural history; perhaps Griffiths will go on to supply the full-scale biographical treatment that is missing here--and that this compelling historical and critical synthesis shows would be more than justified. Upper-division undergraduates through faculty. -- *S. Botterill, University of California, Berkeley*
Review in 2000 Oct CHOICE

THE GEOGRAPHY OF TRANSLATION AND INTERPRETATION: TRAVELING BETWEEN LANGUAGES

by Rainer Schulte

0-7734-7271-1   256pp.   2002

In this very readable book on translation theory, Schulte outlines some of the important steps a translator goes through--both mentally and physically--during the translation process. The title of the book is well chosen, since the author explores the different methods that the translator employs throughout the entire bilingual process, keeping source, target texts, and target audiences in mind. Schulte views every translation as a process that affects both the translator and the target text, and this is the value in his analysis. Though immersed in the process because he himself is a translator, Schulte is able to explain the finer points so that students and other translators can see how he thinks and works. For large collections serving upper-division undergraduates through faculty and professional translators. -- *C. M. DiFranco, SUNY at Binghamton* **Review in 2002 June CHOICE**

WOMEN'S VOICES IN THE FICTION OF ELIZABETH GASKELL (1810-1865)

by Marianne Camus

0-7734-6927-3   312pp.   2002

Scholars have blamed Gaskell for being feminine, a unitarian, and a socialist. Both Edgar Wright (*Mrs. Gaskell*, CH, Apr'66) and W.A. Craik (*Elizabeth Gaskell and the English Provincial Novel*, CH, Jun'75) focus on Gaskell's treatment of everyday Victorian life, religious morality, and regional setting. Like Jennifer Uglow's more balanced biography, *Elizabeth Gaskell: A Habit of Stories* (1993), the present title examines the broader cultural contexts of Gaskell's writing, warning readers of the need for an adequate reading strategy. Contemporaneous critics considered Gaskell provocative because she approached the feminine gender as a social construction. Camus argues that Gaskell used a variety of discourses, e.g., female voices demonstrate passive resistance and the refusal of stereotypes. Gaskell's women are subjects, not objects. Her use of conventional "classic realism" thus subverts the restrictive sphere of women's lives. Camus calls this "preconscious feminism" because it quietly deconstructs male authority, including notions about women's sexuality. Intelligent, accessible, and comprehensive, this examination complements Uglow's biography and provides needed reassessment of this notable Victorian intellectual. **Summing Up:** Recommended. All collections of Victorian culture and fiction. -- *S. A. Parker, emerita, Hiram College*
Review in 2003 Apr CHOICE

A HISTORY OF WOMEN'S CONTRIBUTIONS TO WORLD HEALTH

by Theodora P. Dakin

0-7734-9624-6   128pp.   1992

Dakin ably and concisely fulfills her goal to show that women throughout history have made enormous contributions to health care. No large number of women appear in any one period because of existing social, financial, political, legal, and gender barriers. The aggregate, however, documents that, despite multiple constraints, outstanding women emerged in all periods to become physicians, scientists, surgeons, nurses, and midwives, all of whom cared for people from birth to death. In the Middle Ages midwives held complete monopoly of women's care; men were barred by law from this specialty. Contributions covered many fields: anatomy, physiology, psychiatry, biochemistry, nutrition, and pharmacy. Along the way, Dakin provides an overview of medical history within the milieu characterizing each period. The content in this slim volume arouses the reader's interest and enthusiasm in pursuing more in-depth study. Recommended especially for those in the health professions, science, history, and women's studies. -- *A. R. Davis, U.S. Public Health Service*

Review in 1992 June CHOICE

THE EQUALITY OF THE TWO SEXES

by Poullain de La Barre
Translated by A.D. Frankforter and Paul Morman

0-88946-303-4   150pp.   1989

A translation of the 17th-century Cartesian philosopher
Poulain de la Barre's De l'egalite des deux sexes. The
translator's introduction is useful in putting the work into
context: first, as an attempt by a follower of Descartes to
put the notion of demonstration by "clear and distinct"
ideas into practice by tackling one of the more unques-
tioned assumptions of the age; and second, as an early attempt at formulating arguments in a feminist vein. The
work, however, remains one of limited importance. It is an
interesting historical artifact, but had no impact on the
philosophical debates generated by Cartesianism or the
later feminism. Although it is useful for scholars to have
access to this early exercise in defense of women, the
book is appropriate only for those libraries serving graduate programs in women's studies or European intellectural
history. -- *M. Feder-Marcus, SUNY College at Old West-
bury*
Review in 1990 May CHOICE

MACHADO DE ASSIS AND FEMINISM: RE-READING THE HEART OF THE COMPANION

by Maria Manuel Lisboa

0-7734-8828-6   248pp.   1996

The thesis of Lisboa's study of Brazil's celebrated
Machado de Assis (1839-1908) is that a connection exists
between the Machadean text of the late 19th century and
tenets of 20th-century radical feminist criticism. This line
of inquiry is intended to rescue hitherto unexplored meaning in the novels and thereby add to the view of Machado
as an unorthodox and revolutionary writer. Lisboa's careful explications of the novels reveals an uncanny correspondence between Machado's craft in casting characters
and motives, particularly women and their circumstances,
and contemporary feminist theory. Although the author
clearly and cogently states her position in the areas of both
theory and critical reading of the novels, her main argument, which casts Machado as the author of romans a clef
expounding what would correspond to a radical feminist
program of today, gains in imagination what it lacks in
critical precision and credibility. Given the very ambiguity
of Machado's prose, of which Lisboa is well aware, her
insistence on a feminist reading of texts about weak men
who destroy strong women runs the risk of becoming
more a one-dimensional reductionism than an exploration
of the intriguing and always unexpected modernity of
Machado's genius. Though the book maintains the character and style of a doctoral dissertation, Lisboa writes with
humor, wit, and scholarship. Her book is a knowledgeable
addition to the critical appraisal of a much-neglected literary master. Recommended for graduates, researchers, faculty, and specialists. -- *K. D. Jackson, Yale University*
Review in 1996 Dec CHOICE

WOMEN AND POLITICS IN JAPAN AND KOREA

by Youngtae Shin

0-7734-6374-7   208pp.   2004

Shin seeks to explicate the structural and cultural factors limiting the role of women in Japanese and Korean politics. The distinctive features of her analysis are the selective comparisons between the political experiences of women in these two countries and the link drawn between grassroots movements and the recognition of women's issues and candidates at the national level. Shin concludes that the limited role of women in national politics to date is more the result of cultural attitudes than structural barriers, even as the analysis demonstrates the formidable nature of structural barriers. Thus, the path to more significant roles for women in Japanese and Korean politics is likely to reflect the impact of protest politics at the local and national level and accompanying changes in cultural norms toward a more inclusive decision-making process. **Summing Up:** Highly recommended. Best suited for inclusion in undergraduate libraries with special collections on Asian politics and gender studies. -- *J. M. Peek, Lyon College*
Review in 2005 Jan CHOICE

About The Edwin Mellen Press

- Key Personnel

- Who is Edwin Mellen?

- Purpose and Goals

- Editorial Direction

- Who reviews our books?

- The Adele Mellen Prize

- Author Testimonials

The Edwin Mellen Press is named in honor of Edwin Davis
Mellen (1860–1917), a businessman and philanthropist from
Cambridge, Massachusetts. Mr. Mellen's library and love of
scholarship inspired the vision for this company. His signature
appears on every book published by The Edwin Mellen Press.

Purpose and Goals

The Edwin Mellen Press is an international publisher of scholarly books. The Press was established in 1973 and today publishes over 400 new titles annually.

The Edwin Mellen Press serves the academic community in the following ways:

1. The Press increases the library resources available to scholars by publishing primary sources, monographs, bibliographies, reference works and translations.

2. The Press selects manuscripts for publication solely because of their contribution to scholarship.

3. The Press maintains the integrity of the editorial evaluation process by refusing to accept any grants, subsidies, or payments toward publication.

> "University presses said it was not financially viable to publish all four volumes of my amaNazarite texts. They asked me to reduce the material. So I went to The Edwin Mellen Press which accepted all four volumes and published them without asking for a financial subsidy."
> – *Professor Irving Hexham, University of Calgary*

Editorial Direction

The Edwin Mellen Press was established by university professors acting in an independent capacity. Over the past thirty years, it has been guided by the editorial counsel of many scholars including:

Peter Beyer, University of Ottawa
Robert Boenig, Texas A&M University
Elizabeth Clark, Duke University
Daniel Cohn-Sherbok, University of Wales
Pink Dandelion, Woodbrooke Quaker Center
Rose Duhon-Sells, Southern University
George Grant, Dalhousie University
Maurice Hindle, Open University
Brian Keith-Smith, University of Bristol
Holger Klein, University of Salzburg
Jan Knappert, Antwerp Swahili Institute
Lai Sing Lam, International Biographical Center, Hong Kong
Jean Laporte, University of Notre Dame
Andrew Linzey, Oxford University
Franklin Littell, Conference on the Holocaust & the Churches
Victor Mair, University of Pennsylvania
Guy Mermier, University of Michigan
Eugene O'Brien, University of Limerick
Charles Parsons, University of Cincinnati
Karla Poewe, University of Lethbridge
Jorge Roman-Lagunas, Florida State University
Michael Schuldiner, University of Alaska
Karl Schweizer, New Jersey Institute of Technology
Daniel Strauss, University of the Orange Free State
Florent Tremblay, College Militaire Royal de Saint-Jean
Wolfgang Virmond, Schleiermacherforschungsstelle Berlin

and many others to whom we are extremely grateful.

"The scholarly standards and requirements of The Edwin Mellen Press are fully as stringent as those of the university presses I have worked with during the thirty-two years of my publishing career."
– Professor Rebecca (R.W.) Crump,
Louisiana StateUniversity

Journal Reviews

Books by The Edwin Mellen Press have been reviewed
by a large number of international scholarly journals, including:
- American Reference Books Annual
- Translation Review
- American Anthropologist
- Journal of Early Modern History
- Sixteenth Century Journal
- Australian Journal of Political Science
- British Journal of Middle Eastern Studies
- Canadian Journal of African Studies
- South African Historical Journal
- China Review International
- Journal of the American Oriental Society
- Journal of Hellenic Studies
- Bulletin of Hispanic Studies
- Journal of Modern Italian Studies
- South European Society and Politics
- International Journal of Iberian Studies
- The French Review
- The Polish Review
- Modern Language Review
- Classical and Modern Literature
- British Association for Romantic Studies
- Shakespeare Bulletin
- American Literary Scholarship
- Western American Literature
- Nineteenth Century Music Review
- The Early Drama, Art and Music Review
- Animations: A Review of Puppetry and Related Theatre
- Asian Theatre Journal
- British Society of Aesthetics
- Transactions of the Charles S. Peirce Society
- International Review of Education
- Journal of Higher Education
- Oxford Journal of Theological Studies
- Journal of the American Academy of Religion
- Journal for the Scientific Study of Religion
- The Catholic Biblical Quarterly
- Conservative Judaism
- International Review of Social History
- International Migration Review
- European Journal of Social Work
- The Journal of the Cricket Society

The Adele Mellen Prize

The Edwin Mellen Press publishes over 400 titles each year. From these, a dozen are awarded the Adele Mellen Prize for their especially distinguished contribution to scholarship. The 2004 selections are:

TRANCE AND TRANSFORMATION OF THE ACTOR IN JAPANESE NOH AND BALINESE MASKED DANCE-DRAMA *by Margaret Coldiron* (University of London, U.K.)

THE RULE OF LAW AND THE LAW OF WAR: MILITARY COMMISSIONS AND ENEMY COMBATANTS POST 9/11 *by Leonard Cutler* (Siena College)

DEVELOPING THE WHOLE CHILD—THE NEED FOR BALANCE IN EARLY YEARS EDUCATION AND CARE *by Mary Katherine Daly* (University College Cork, Ireland)

EPITAPH CULTURE IN THE WEST: VARIATIONS ON A THEME IN CULTURAL HISTORY *by Karl Guthke* (Harvard University)

THE ATLANTA URBAN LEAGUE, 1920–2000 *by Alton Hornsby, Jr.* (Morehouse College) & *Alexa Benson Henderson* (Clark Atlanta University)

INCEST AND INBREEDING AVOIDANCE: A CRITIQUE OF DARWINIAN SOCIAL SCIENCE *by Gregory C. Leavitt* (Idaho State University)

MODELS AND MEANINGS IN THE HISTORY OF JEWISH LEADERSHIP *by Hal Lewis* (Spertus Institute of Jewish Studies)

NATHANIEL HAWTHORNE'S *THE SCARLET LETTER*: A CRITICAL RESOURCE GUIDE & COMPREHENSIVE ANNOTATED BIBLIOGRAPHY OF LITERARY CRITICISM 1950–2000 *by Kimberly Free Muirhead* (Duquesne University)

DEFINING INDIGENEITY IN THE TWENTY-FIRST CENTURY – A CASE STUDY OF THE FRISIANS *by Andrys Onsman* (Monash University, Australia)

AN ENGLISH TRANSLATION OF BACHOFEN'S MUTTERRECHT (MOTHER RIGHT) (1861): A STUDY OF THE RELIGIOUS AND JURIDICAL ASPECTS OF GYNECOCRACY IN THE ANCIENT WORLD (5 Volumes) *by David Partenheimer* (Truman State University)

LUTHER AND CALVIN ON OLD TESTAMENT NARRATIVES: REFORMATION THOUGHT AND NARRATIVE TEXT *by Michael Parsons* (Baptist Theological College, Australia)

RURAL MICROFINANCE IN ARGENTINA AFTER THE TEQUILA CRISIS *by Mark Schreiner* (Washington University in St. Louis)

A SELECTED SOCIO-LEGAL BIBLIOGRAPHY ON ETHNIC CLEANSING, WARTIME RAPE, AND GENOCIDE IN THE FORMER YUGOSLAVIA AND RWANDA *by Hilmi M. Zawati* (Bishop's University, Canada) *and Ibtisam M. Mahmoud* (Montreal Documentation Library of Rights and Democracy)

Author Testimonials